MW01284070

THE FEDERALIST

Excerpts with Commentary

2nd edition

By

James Madison

Alexander Hamilton

John Jay

Commentary by

Roderick Saxey, MD

Edited by

Lisa Saxey

Haus Sachse Enterprises, Inc.

Edmonds, Washington

Copyright 2015

by Roderick Saxey, MD

ISBN-13: 978-0997018103
ISBN-10: 0997018100

Also by Dr. Saxey, available at Amazon.com:

***All Enlisted, A Mormon Missionary in Austria
During the Vietnam Era***

Blog site:

http://docsaxey.com

For God, Family, and Country

Concerning Format

THE FEDERALIST was published as a series of numbered essays or papers. Each excerpt reproduced here is preceded by the number in Roman numerals (I, II, III . . .) of the paper from which it is taken and by the title of the essay in all capitals. Original spelling and punctuation are preserved.

Commentaries are preceded by the number of the paper in Arabic numerals (1, 2, 3 . . .) with a heading to indicate the topic of modern interest to which the excerpt pertains.

Contents

INTRODUCTION

Ours is an age of continued constitutional crisis: the "Imperial Presidency" that so troubled the pundits in the early 1970s ripened to a fullness in the Executive Orders and presidential disregard for law of the 2010s, while the "Imperial Congress" described in the 1990s by the Heritage Foundation weakened to an ineffectual stew of special interests, careerists, and political hacks. The executive and legislative branches of our government have always been and are designed to be in a condition of tense equilibrium that alternately favors one or the other, but this seems in our age to have become a gyration of extremes. We then add judicial activism to the mix, with the Supreme Court and other courts creating new law out of thin air often in blatant disregard for the expressed will of the people. But I refer to a more fundamental constitutional crisis, namely a lack of understanding by the people of the basic objectives and limitations of the American system of government. The solution to this crisis is education, and what better source material for that education than the works of the founding fathers themselves?

THE FEDERALIST was written in 1787 and 1788 by James Madison, Alexander Hamilton, and John Jay as a series of newspaper articles to refute criticisms of the proposed Constitution. They were meant to explain more clearly to the people how the new government would work and how its powers would be restricted so as to preserve the freedoms that had been so recently asserted by force of arms and the shedding of blood, and to explain why and how the new government would correct the deficiencies of the failed federal government under the previous Articles of Confederation.

It is natural that an attempt to renew constitutional government in our day should turn to THE FEDERALIST for understanding and instruction. For although some modern lawyers seem to think it and other writings by the founders are their private preserve, THE FEDERALIST in fact was written for general publication, to persuade the public to vote for the Constitution. The Constitution was meant to be read and understood by every voter.

But, alas, the average citizen's attention span in 1787 was much longer than it is today, and the level of literacy was higher. (A nationwide survey in the early 1990s showed 40% functional illiteracy among adults and conditions have not improved since then; American literacy at the time of Thomas Jefferson has been estimated between 90% and 95%.) Even for the educated modern reader THE FEDERALIST can be difficult, written as it is in sometimes turgid eighteenth century legal and philosophical language.

Nevertheless, many passages are perfectly clear, often eloquent, prompting Jefferson to refer to it as the "best commentary on the principles of government ever written." It may come as a surprise to those reading the words of the founders for the first time that their ideas are so contemporary, as if prepared for this week's op-ed page or the latest tweet. This testifies to their insight, experience, wisdom, and inspiration, as well as to the universality and persistence of the problems of government and society they addressed.

This work is offered as a help for finding some of those "best" passages which are particularly pertinent to our modern condition. It consists of a series of excerpts only and is certainly no substitute for the original text and context; the exquisite logic and carefully constructed arguments of the complete work will delight and inspire the serious student. My own commentary is that of a layman, neither lawyer nor politician, but an ordinary voter like those for whom THE FEDERALIST was written.

There is great discontent in America. Much of that discontent can be reduced by reestablishing the proper relationship between government and citizen, a relationship based on the founders' vision of limited, unobtrusive government created by free men and women who assume individual responsibility for their lives.

THE FEDERALIST

I. GENERAL INTRODUCTION

To the People of the State of New York:

After an unequivocal experience of the inefficiency of the subsisting federal government, you are called upon to deliberate on a new Constitution for the United States of America. The subject speaks its own importance; comprehending in its consequences nothing less than the existence of the **UNION**, the safety and welfare of the parts of which it is composed, the fate of an empire in many respects the most interesting in the world. It has been frequently remarked that it seems to have been reserved to the people of this country, by their conduct and example, to decide the important question, whether societies of men are really capable or not of establishing good government from reflection and choice, or whether they are forever destined to depend for their political constitutions on accident and force. If there be any truth in the remark, the crisis at which we are arrived may with propriety be regarded as the era in which that decision is to be made; and a wrong election of the part we shall act may, in this view, deserve to be considered as the general misfortune of mankind. . . .

Were there not even inducements to moderation, nothing could be more ill-judged than that intolerant spirit which has, at all times, characterized political parties. For in politics, as in religion, it is equally absurd to aim at making proselytes by fire and sword. Heresies in either can rarely be cured by persecution.

1. The Importance of the American Experiment

The founding fathers were acutely aware of the significance of their actions, not only for themselves and their posterity, but for the entire world. It is a tribute to their greatness as well as to their necessity that they generally overcame the temptation to pursue individual or party interests. They blended the spirit of rigid adherence to principles of individual liberty with the spirit of mutual accommodation to establish a "new order" of things, and they did this without the bloodshed that had characterized all such prior transitions.

I. GENERAL INTRODUCTION

(A) dangerous ambition more often lurks behind the specious mask of zeal for the rights of the people than under the forbidding appearance of zeal for the firmness and efficiency of government.

History will teach us that the former has been found a much more certain road to the introduction of despotism than the latter, and that of those men who have overturned the liberties of republics, the greatest number have begun heir career by paying an obsequious court to the people; commencing demagogues, and ending tyrants.

1. Demagoguery

The wisdom of this observation was verified again with the French Revolution in 1789, the same year the Constitution was adopted, as well as on many occasions since that time, most notably in the 20th century with its varied socialist regimes, many ironically named "peoples'" republics. The diligent student may profitably review in this context George Orwell's brilliant little book, *Animal Farm*, noting the portentous year of publication, 1945.

II. CONCERNING DANGERS FROM FOREIGN FORCE AND INFLUENCE

. . . Providence has been pleased to give this one connected country to one united people--a people descended from the same ancestors, speaking the same language, professing the same religion, attached to the same principles of government, very similar in their manners and customs, and who, by their joint counsels, arms, and efforts, fighting side by side throughout a long and bloody war, have nobly established general liberty and independence.

2. Multiculturalism

The United States was founded by people who, for all their differences, thought of themselves as having a common culture, with the laws growing out of that culture. As others have migrated to this country they have been warmly welcomed, and, in the course of a generation or two they have adopted American culture, becoming in the process Americans. That never meant rejecting completely their Old World traditions, only that those traditions became family traditions rather than national ones. It is a serious mistake to suppose that a stable social and political system can exist or long endure which does not require all its members to use a common language, common customs, and common moral principles, in short, the common culture of received tradition. All previous attempts at such unequal unions have failed or been continued only through sacrifice of liberty. In short, "multiculturalism" is a mistake.

III. CONCERNING DANGERS FROM FOREIGN FORCE AND INFLUENCE

The pride of states, as well as of men, naturally disposes them to justify all their actions, and opposes their acknowledging, correcting, or repairing their errors and offences. The national government, in such cases, will not be affected by this pride, but will proceed with moderation and candor to consider and decide on the means most proper to extricate them from the difficulties which threaten them.

3. Arrogance in Government

At the time of the Constitutional Convention there was great concern that conflicts between the states could result in warfare, instigated or encouraged by European or other powers. It was hoped that the federal government could prevent this, a hope which with the exception of the Civil War has been justified. We now live in a time, however, when the "pride of states" has become a national affliction particularly characteristic of the national government, as demonstrated by endless persistence of counterproductive programs (Nobel laureate Milton Friedman once remarked, "Nothing is so permanent as a temporary government program.") and by arrogance of both elected officials and unelected bureaucrats, the latter often functioning in agencies of dubious constitutional validity. The comedian who says, "We're from the government and we're here to help," elicits as many sneers and groans as laughs.

X. THE UNION AS A SAFEGUARD AGAINST DOMESTIC FACTION AND INSURRECTION

Among the numerous advantages promised by a well-constructed union, none deserves to be more accurately developed than its tendency to break and control the violence of faction . . . measures are too often decided, not according to the rules of justice and the rights of the minor party, but by the superior force of an interested and overbearing majority. . . .

(There are a) prevailing and increasing distrust of public engagements, and alarm for private rights, which are echoed from one end of the continent to the other. These must be chiefly, if not wholly, effects of the unsteadiness and injustice with which a factious spirit has tainted our public administrations.

10. Distrust of Government

The increased wealth of our country over the last two hundred fifty years has permitted the proliferation of special interest groups, often devoted to the promotion of a single political issue. While these serve a purpose in teaching about their individual causes, they tend to err on the side of over-educated ignorance, missing the broader picture of right and wrong, the preservation of liberty, and the rule of law. They not only lose perspective, they do it with zeal. Our numerous media likewise contribute to the sense of "alarm." Just as this was related by

Madison to the "unsteadiness and injustice (of) . . . our public administrations" in his day, so likewise rank partisanship and administrative incompetence and inconsistency must be held accountable for this condition now.

X. THE UNION AS A SAFEGUARD AGAINST DOMESTIC FACTION AND INSURRECTION

It is in vain to say that enlightened statesmen will be able to adjust these clashing interests, and render them all subservient to the public good. Enlightened statesmen will not always be at the helm. . . .

(W)e well know that neither moral nor religious motives can be relied on as an adequate control. . . .

(A) pure democracy . . . can admit of no cure for the mischiefs of faction . . . such democracies have ever been spectacles of turbulence and contention; have ever been found incompatible with personal security or the rights of property; and have in general been as short in their lives as they have been violent in their deaths.

A republic, by which I mean a government in which the scheme of representation takes place, opens a different prospect, and promises the cure for which we are seeking.

10. Failings of Democracy

America has been blessed with numerous instances when "enlightened statesmen" have occupied the highest offices of our country, but there have been many more instances when this was not the case. As indicated in this quotation, the more closely a political system approaches pure democracy, the less likely it will be able to preserve itself with any degree of stability. The Constitution is designed to avoid the pitfalls of democracy while preserving the democratic voice of the people through their elected representatives. A common error has been to confuse freedom with democracy, but freedom may exist under a wide variety of political systems, and may disappear in a democracy. The founding fathers were concerned to avoid the evils both of rule by few and of rule by many.

XI. THE UTILITY OF THE UNION IN RESPECT TO COMMERCIAL RELATIONS AND A NAVY

Every institution will grow and flourish in proportion to the quantity and extent of the means concentred toward its formation and support.

11. The Failure of the Welfare State

This comment was made with reference to providing adequate funds for a national navy, but it is

18

a general principle with wide applicability. If an activity is subsidized, that activity increases. Thus, providing increased support to unwed mothers has been accompanied by a dramatic increase in the number of unwed mothers (from 5.3% in 1960 to 28.0% in 1990). A corollary is that applying penalties to something results in less of it. This is most glaring in the tax code, where, for instance, taxation of capital investment and savings has contributed to an abysmal national savings rate.

XII. THE UTILITY OF THE UNION IN RESPECT TO REVENUE

The prosperity of commerce is now perceived and acknowledged by all enlightened statesmen to be the most useful as well as the most productive source of national wealth, and has accordingly become a primary object of their political cares . . .

The ability of a country to pay taxes must always be proportioned, in a great degree, to the quantity of money in circulation, and to the celerity with which it circulates . . .

It is evident from the state of the country, from the habits of the people, from the experience we have had on the point itself, that it is impracticable to raise any very considerable sums by direct taxation. Tax laws have in vain been multiplied; new methods to enforce the collection have in vain been tried; the public expectation has been uniformly disappointed, and the treasuries of the States have remained empty.

12. Trade, Taxation, and Economic Policy

The principles of "supply side" economics go back far beyond the 1980s, as documented by Professor Charles Adams in his book, *For Good and Evil.* Already in 1788 the states had noted the diligence and cleverness of the citizenry in avoiding taxes. It was concluded that the new federal government should raise its revenue through tariffs, excises, and dues from the individual state governments, but the correct apportionment of these was a matter of great concern and debate (see next section). Experience under the Articles of Confederation taught that state dues were an unreliable source of funds. Federal policy, therefore, as well as that of the states, was meant to encourage the unhindered growth of commerce, for that increasing economic activity would lead not only to the enriching of individuals, but also to the creation of wealth for the government through taxation.

XII. THE UTILITY OF THE UNION IN RESPECT TO REVENUE

Revenue, therefore, must be had at all events. In this country, if the principal part be not drawn from commerce, it must fall with oppressive weight upon land. It has been already intimated that excises, in their true signification, are too little in unison with the feelings of the people, to admit of great use being made of that mode of taxation . . . Personal estate . . . cannot be subjected to large contributions, by any other means than by taxes on consumption.

12. Modes of Taxation

Modern experience with tariffs and excise taxes has confirmed that they are restrictive on trade--some of the most successful economies of recent decades have done away with tariffs altogether. Tariffs continue in this country more as part of the executive's "trade sanctions" to punish foreign governments than as a significant source of revenue. In fact, they often end up harming American companies and consumers more than anyone else.

Note the last line in this quotation, that successful taxes should be based on consumption. A more fair and equitable distribution of tax burden than that which now exists could be accomplished by applying this principle in the form of a national transaction or sales tax. This would avoid the complexity and injustice of the income tax and trade-restrictive effects of tariffs.

XIV. OBJECTIONS TO THE PROPOSED CONSTITUTION FROM EXTENT OF TERRITORY ANSWERED

In the first place it is to be remembered that the general government is not to be charged with the whole power of making and administering laws. Its jurisdiction is limited to certain enumerated objects, which concern all the members of the republic, but which are not to be attained by the separate provisions of any. The subordinate governments, which can extend their care to all those other objects which can be separately provided for, will retain their due authority and activity.

14. Limited Government

This principle, that the federal government is to have limited powers, is the most abused and ignored concept in American history. The Civil War firmly established the authority of the central government over the states insofar as the integrity of the Union is concerned, but it was the creation of the welfare state under Franklin D. Roosevelt with its subsequent dramatic expansions under Lyndon Johnson, Bill Clinton, the Bushes, and now Barack Obama, that have constituted the de facto rejection of federal limits. And yet there is probably no more important concept in the Constitution than this, that government must be limited in its activity, authority, and scope, performing only those functions specifically delegated to it by the people, for all power and authority reside ultimately with them. It is the great challenge of our generation peacefully to re-establish this principle; otherwise, its abrogation shall represent nullification of the Constitution itself, hence loss of federal legitimacy.

XVII. THE INSUFFICIENCY OF THE PRESENT CONFEDERATION TO PRESERVE THE UNION

The administration of private justice between the citizens of the same State, the supervision of agriculture and of other concerns of a similar nature, all those things, in short, which are proper to be provided for by local legislation, can never be desirable cares of a general jurisdiction. It is therefore improbable that there should exist a disposition in the federal councils to usurp the powers with which they are connected; because the attempt to exercise those powers would be as troublesome as it would be nugatory; and the possession of them, for that reason, would contribute nothing to the dignity, to the importance, or to the splendor of the national government.

But let it be admitted, for argument's sake, that mere wantonness and lust of domination would be sufficient to beget that disposition; still it may be safely affirmed, that the sense of the constituent body of the national representatives, or, in other words, the people of the several States, would control the indulgence of so extravagant an appetite. It will always be far more easy for the State governments to encroach upon the national authorities, than for the national government to encroach upon the State authorities . . .

(T)hey (the separate state governments) will generally possess the confidence and good-will of the people, and with so important a support, will be able effectually to oppose all encroachments of the national government.

17. Limited Government, States' Rights

Mr. Hamilton was overly optimistic. Looking back on the failure of the government created by the Articles of Confederation and seeing the need for a stronger central government, he could not foresee it intruding into private life to the degree that modern technology has permitted. Nor did he predict such a loss of understanding of and faith in the Constitution that now exist following nearly a century of false philosophy and poor education. The national government has indeed extended its care far beyond matters of "general jurisdiction." It was hoped that the states would control the national government in its attempts to usurp power, but this has not been successful. Particularly since the Great Depression, many state governments have become willing accomplices to Washington and have looked to it for solutions to problems which should be and in an earlier time were handled at local levels.

XVIII. THE INSUFFICIENCY OF THE PRESENT CONFEDERATION TO PRESERVE THE UNION

As a weak government, when not at war, is ever agitated by internal dissensions, so these never fail to bring on fresh calamities from abroad.

18. Foreign Intervention

This observation means that foreign powers would take advantage of weak and divided governments. No doubt true, as exemplified by deteriorating international conditions in the current century. But the principle also has been turned around by various presidents, who, unable to solve political squabbles or to reconcile domestic inconsistencies, have looked abroad for foreign policy success to improve their popularity, even when this has required military action and loss of life.

XXI. OTHER DEFECTS OF THE PRESENT CONFEDERATION

(T)here can be no common measure of national wealth, and, of course, no general or stationary rule by which the ability of a state to pay taxes can be determined. . . .

Imposts, excises, and, in general, all duties upon articles of consumption, may be compared to a fluid, which will, in time, find its level with the means of paying them. The amount to be contributed by each citizen will in a degree be at his own option, and can be regulated by an attention to his resources. . . .

It is a signal advantage of taxes on articles of consumption, that they contain in their own nature a security against excess. They prescribe their own limit; which cannot be exceeded without defeating the end proposed,--that is, an extension of the revenue. When applied to this object, the saying is as just as it is witty, that, "in political arithmetic, two and two do not always make four." If duties are too high, they lessen the consumption; the collection is eluded; and the product to the treasury is not so great as when they are confined within proper and moderate bounds. This forms a complete barrier against any material oppression of the citizens by taxes of this class, and is itself a natural limitation of the power of imposing them.

21. Taxation

Here we have an excellent argument in favor of some sort of national sales tax. In the years of the

Continental Congress, national revenue was obtained by imposing dues on the member states. The states frequently defaulted on their payments, so it was recognized that the new national government would likewise have difficulty raising funds if based on state requisitions. The author's description of an automatic feedback mechanism (an Invisible Hand of taxes) has been confirmed in various settings, notably the income tax. Whether rates are high or low, actual taxes collected by this system total about 18-19% of Gross Domestic Product.

What does change with the tax rate is the total GDP itself--high tax rates discourage economic activity, retard economic growth, and drive the GDP down, while low tax rates stimulate the economy and drive GDP up. Thus we have the apparent paradox of declining revenues in the wake of increased tax rates. (Members of Congress have the darnedest time understanding this, but it is quite sensible to any business owner who has decided to hire part-time rather than full-time employees or contractors instead of employees in order to avoid paying benefits and payroll taxes, or a student who mows lawns for cash only, or a homemaker who has decided to shop elsewhere when her usual store raises its prices.)

XXII. OTHER DEFECTS OF THE PRESENT CONFEDERATION

(T)he fundamental maxim of republican government (requires) that the sense of the majority should prevail.

22. Representative Democracy

It is a peculiarity of the late twentieth and early twenty-first century, and a testimony to the corruption of our current system of districting and elections, that the "sense of the majority" frequently does not prevail even though the government maintains the semblance of representation. Every ten years the congressional districts are re-drawn to reflect population growth and changes in people's geographic distribution. Gerrymandering is the process of drawing legislative district boundaries in a bizarre, wandering illogical manner so as to increase the likelihood of a particular party being elected, without regard to other legal, physical, or social borders. The gerrymander is intended specifically to "go around" the majority of voters by creating "safe" districts, thus subverting the sense of the majority.

XXII. OTHER DEFECTS OF THE PRESENT CONFEDERATION

The organization of Congress is itself utterly improper for the exercise of those powers which are necessary to be deposited in the Union. A single assembly may be a proper receptacle of those slender, or rather fettered, authorities, which have been heretofore delegated to the federal head; but it would be inconsistent with all the principles of good government, to intrust it with those additional powers which, even the moderate and more rational adversaries of the proposed Constitution admit, ought to reside in the United States. If that plan should not be adopted, and if the necessity of the Union should be able to withstand the ambitious aims of those men who may indulge magnificent schemes of personal aggrandizement from its dissolution, the probability would be, that we should run into the project in conferring supplementary powers upon Congress, as they are now constituted; and either the machine, from the intrinsic feebleness of its structure, will moulder into pieces, in spite of our ill-judged efforts to prop it; or, by successive augmentations of its force and energy, as necessity might prompt, we shall finally accumulate, in a single body, all the most important prerogatives of sovereignty, and thus entail upon our posterity one of the most execrable forms of government that human infatuation ever contrived. Thus we should create in reality that very tyranny which the adversaries of the new Constitution either are, or affect to be, solicitous to avert.

22. Tyranny

The congress referred to in this paragraph is, of course, the unicameral government that existed prior to adoption of the Constitution. It is important to note the danger warned of by the author of accumulating excessive power in one institution. This was avoided in those days; has it happened now, over two centuries later?

XXII. OTHER DEFECTS OF THE PRESENT CONFEDERATION

The fabric of American empire ought to rest on the solid basis of THE CONSENT OF THE PEOPLE. The streams of national power ought to flow immediately from that pure, original fountain of all legitimate authority.

XXV. THE POWERS NECESSARY TO THE COMMON DEFENCE FURTHER CONSIDERED

Wise politicians will be cautious about fettering the government with restrictions that cannot be observed, because they know that every breach of the fundamental laws, though dictated by necessity, impairs that sacred reverence which ought to be maintained in the breast of rulers toward the constitution of a country, and forms a precedent for other breaches where the same plea of necessity does not exist at all, or is less urgent and palpable.

22. and 25. Tyranny and the Consent of the People

The importance of the willingness of the people to consent to the laws of the nation cannot be over-emphasized. As Jefferson put it in the Declaration of Independence, governments derive their "just powers from the consent of the governed." The genius of the American system of government is that it enables, or should enable, the people to vote out of office those individuals who act in a manner to which the people do not consent. Regulations which diminish the power of the people to express or withhold their consent are contrary to that genius. Greater than 90% re-election rates and divided governments in which conservative candidates for president win landslides while liberal congressmen are re-elected to majority control (or vice-versa) are symptomatic of a skewed system, one which no longer clearly expresses the voice of the people, notwithstanding the tortured reasoning of pundits trying to explain it.

It is essential that government officials conduct themselves in obedience to the Constitution and other laws of the land. The assertion that the Constitution is a "living, breathing, document" is foolish fantasy, ridiculous rhetoric designed to conceal caprice and the imposition of personal will. That the Constitution can be changed is true; there are provisions within it to do just that. But inasmuch as the branches of government or their agents have conducted themselves contrary to the meaning of Constitutional provisions as generally understood by the ordinary citizen, they have reduced the value of those fundamental laws, decreased the likelihood that ordinary citizens will find it edifying to obey the law, and greatly diminished their own authority in office.

XXVIII. THE IDEA OF RESTRAINING THE LEGISLATIVE AUTHORITY IN REGARD TO THE COMMON DEFENCE CONSIDERED

If the representatives of the people betray their constituents, there is then no resource left but in the exertion of that original right of self-defence which is paramount to all positive forms of government, and which against the usurpations of the national rulers, may be exerted with infinitely better prospect of success than against those of the rulers of the individual state.

28. Civil Disobedience

Thomas Jefferson suggested that it was good for society to have a little rebellion now and then. (Not, we might add, the continual revolution of Marxist theory.) Here the authors of the Constitution are more explicit, rebellion being appropriately directed toward unfaithful stewards.

XXVIII. THE IDEA OF RESTRAINING THE LEGISLATIVE AUTHORITY IN REGARD TO THE COMMON DEFENCE CONSIDERED

The obstacles to usurpation and the facilities of resistance increase with the increased extent of the state, provided the citizens understand their rights and are disposed to defend them.

28. Individual Liberty

Modern technology has decreased the value of territorial extent as an obstacle to the excessive accumulation of power in the federal government. But the willingness of the citizens to protect their own freedom has always been the more important factor. The potential enemy of that freedom is identified here as the central authority.

XXVIII. THE IDEA OF RESTRAINING THE LEGISLATIVE AUTHORITY IN REGARD TO THE COMMON DEFENCE CONSIDERED

It may safely be received as an axiom in our political system that the State governments will, in all possible contingencies, afford complete security against invasions of the public liberty by the national authority. Projects of usurpation cannot be masked under pretences so likely to escape the penetration of select bodies of men, as of the people at large.

28. States' Rights

The state governments are key bulwarks of freedom against the encroachments of Washington. Their frequent failures in this regard may be traced to the Civil War, remembered still in some areas as the failed "War for Southern Independence." State authority declined further in the mistaken attempt by Southern Democrats to defend the indefensible practices of discrimination and segregation during the 1960s. Nevertheless, the principle that state governments have an obligation to restrict the power of the federal government (and not usually the other way around) remains valid. It is up to our generation to reinvigorate the power of the states to accomplish this purpose. Nullification--the refusal by some states to refuse to act on unfunded federal mandates or comply with unconstitutional federal regulations--is a step in the right direction.

XXIX. CONCERNING THE MILITIA

(The national) army can never by formidable to the liberties of the people while there is a large body of citizens little, if at all, inferior to them in discipline and the use of arms, who stand ready to defend their own rights and those of their fellow citizens.

29. Gun Control

There are those who argue that the right to bear arms pertains only to the organized militia or National Guard, and that the second amendment has been obviated by modern military conditions. But *militia* in 1788 meant simply the sum of able-bodied male citizens, all or nearly all of whom were assumed to be able to bear arms. (Hunting for subsistence or pleasure has no part in the discussion at all.) Mr. Hamilton makes it clear in this statement and elsewhere in THE FEDERALIST that the significance of an armed citizenry is in its ability to defend itself not against foreign powers but against the federal government itself. It is, in other words, one of the famous checks and balances necessary for the proper regulation of government.

XXXI. CONCERNING THE GENERAL POWER OF TAXATION

It is, therefore, as necessary that the State governments should be able to command the means of supplying their wants, as that the national government should possess the like faculty with respect to the wants of the Union. But an indefinite power of taxation in the *latter* might, and probably would in time, deprive the *former* of the means of providing for their own necessities; and would subject them entirely to the mercy of the national legislature.

31. Taxation

It is repeatedly noted that the federal government shall not have an indefinite (unlimited) power of taxation. Here the reason for this limitation is that if the federal government consumes available tax dollars then there will be so many the fewer for state purposes. Thus, the states would become obligated to the federal government for their support. This is exactly what has happened and is illustrated every time a governor, or worse yet a mayor, appeals to Washington for a subsidy. Even the benign-appearing "revenue sharing" is but an inefficient diversion of resources from private, local, and state hands through Washington, increasing in the process the power of the central government and diminishing that of everyone else.

XXXI. CONCERNING THE GENERAL POWER OF TAXATION

This mode of reasoning appears sometimes to turn upon the supposition of usurpation in the national government . . . The moment we launch into conjectures about the usurpations of the federal government, we get into an unfathomable abyss, and fairly put ourselves out of the reach of all reasoning. Imagination may range at pleasure . . . In what does our security consist against usurpation from that quarter? Doubtless in the manner of their formation and in a due dependence of those who are to administer them upon the people. If the proposed construction of the federal government be found, upon an impartial examination of it, to be such as to afford to a proper extent, the same species of security (as in the state governments), all apprehensions on the score of usurpation ought to be discarded.

31. Limited Government

The federalists were at great pains to reassure everyone that the national government would not, could not, become tyrannical.

XXXII. CONCERNING THE GENERAL POWER OF TAXATION

But as the plan of the convention aims only at a partial union or consolidation, the State governments would clearly retain all the rights of sovereignty which they before had, and which were not, by that act, *exclusively* delegated to the United States. This exclusive delegation, or rather this alienation, of State sovereignty, would only exist in three cases: where the Constitution in express terms granted an exclusive authority to the Union; where it granted in one instance an authority to the Union and in another prohibited the States from exercising the like authority; and where it granted an authority to the Union to which a similar authority in the States would be absolutely and totally *contradictory* and *repugnant*.

32. Limited Government

While it is true that the Constitution and the "plan of the convention" intended only a partial union, the Civil War made clear that the union is indissoluble unless pursued by amendment or mutual agreement. This does not mean, however, that whenever there is an issue between the federal government and the states or individuals, the latter must always lose. Nevertheless, it has been the practice of the Supreme Court for many decades to almost always rule in favor of greater federal power.

XXXIII. CONCERNING THE GENERAL POWER OF TAXATION

(T)he danger which most threatens our political welfare is that the State governments will finally sap the foundations of the Union . . .

The propriety of a law, in a constitutional light, must always be determined by the nature of the powers upon which it is founded.

33. Limited Government

This was a legitimate concern in the minds of the founding fathers as they tried to bring a single government to thirteen squabbling states, but as frankly settled with the Civil War; it has been observed that the *United States* as a noun took a plural verb before 1861 but was singular after 1865. Antebellum federalism was diminished and we entered a golden age of national republican government, a golden age which ended sometime between Wilsonian internationalism and the New Deal, that is, with the arrival to power of the so-called "Progressives." Massive expansion of the national government since then has resulted in a union bearing no resemblance to that envisioned in this quotation. The states and their citizens now confront Leviathan.

All laws (and regulations with the force of law, but written by unknown, unaccountable, and unelected bureaucrats) must be clearly based on principles in the Constitution. When Supreme Court justices base judgments on "adumbrations of emanations" from the Constitution, they not only prove their foolishness in the eyes of the people, but undermine the rule of law generally.

XXXIV. CONCERNING THE GENERAL POWER OF TAXATION

(I)n a short course of time, the wants of the States will naturally reduce themselves within *a very narrow compass*: and in the interim, the United States will, in all probability, find it convenient to abstain wholly from those objects to which the particular States would be inclined to resort.

34. Limited Government

THE FEDERALIST correctly notes that the states would be reduced in their interests, but the United States has shown little interest or ability to "abstain" from state or even local issues, going so far in recent years as to dictate details of local zoning and school financing.

XXXV. CONCERNING THE GENERAL POWER OF TAXATION

(A)ll extremes are pernicious in various ways. Exorbitant duties on imported articles would beget a general spirit of smuggling   . . .

35. Government Policy and Moral Philosophy

The first statement in this quotation is a general principle of virtue with widespread applicability in life. The second refers to only one of many ill-effects of protectionist trade practices and excessive taxation.

XXXV. CONCERNING THE GENERAL POWER OF TAXATION

Necessity, especially in politics, often occasions false hopes, false reasoning, and a system of measures correspondingly erroneous . . .

The idea of an actual representation of all classes of the people by persons of each class, is altogether visionary. Unless it were expressly provided in the Constitution, that each different occupation should send one or more member, the thing would never take place in practice . . .

We must therefore consider merchants the natural representatives of all these classes of the community . . .

It is said to be necessary, that all classes of citizens should have some of their own number in the representative body, in order that their feelings and interests may be the better understood and attended to. But we have seen that this will never happen under any arrangement that leaves the votes of the people free.

35. Proportional Representation

The idea that the populace must be broken down into various subgroups (by social class, occupation, ethnic group, or some other criterion) found currency in Europe under the label of "proportional representation." It is in fact enforced affirmative action applied to the political arena. The founders correctly observed that any such proportionality must of necessity infringe on the power of the people to choose their representatives by majority vote.

XXXV. CONCERNING THE GENERAL POWER OF TAXATION

This dependence (on fellow citizens for their votes), and the necessity of being bound himself, and his posterity, by the laws to which he gives assent, are the true, and they are the strong chords of sympathy between the representative and the constituent.

35. Corruption and the Imperial Congress

In the modern era Congress routinely exempts

itself from the laws it passes. This may have made some sense in rare times and circumstances past, the justification being to avoid limiting the power of Congress, but in those days congressmen usually left Congress after a term or a few terms and then were subject to the laws they had passed. With 90-98% reelection rates and political careers routinely extending for thirty, forty, or more years, a new "class" has been created, one which is not bound by the laws which bind the balance of the people. This ruling class, the so-called *elite*, has all the arrogance of Old World aristocracy but none of its virtue.

XXXVI. CONCERNING THE GENERAL POWER OF TAXATION

(W)hether the representation of the people be more or less numerous, it will consist almost entirely of proprietors of land, of merchants, and of members of the learned professions, who will truly represent all those different interests and views . . . There are strong minds in every walk of life that will rise superior to the disadvantages of situation, and will command the tribute due to their merit, not only from the classes to which they particularly belong, but from the society in general. The door ought to be equally open to all . . .

36. Term Limits

It was anticipated that a broad cross-section of Americans with a wide variety of experience, knowledge, and skill would serve in government, but that most would be large farmers, businessmen, teachers, physicians, lawyers, and a sprinkling of others. Now, however, the vast majority of our elected officials are lawyers turned professional politicians. Mandatory rotation of the individuals in office could help reduce this imbalance of experience and interest in our elected officials. (Also, there is an inherent conflict of interest in having practicing lawyers serve in the legislature where they determine the nature of the rules under which, and confirm judges before whom, they or their partners must argue cases.)

XXXVI. CONCERNING THE GENERAL POWER OF TAXATION

It has been very properly observed by different speakers and writers on the side of the Constitution, that if the exercise of the power of internal taxation by the Union should be discovered on experiment to be really inconvenient, the federal government may then forbear the use of it, and have recourse to requisitions in its stead . . .

When the particular debts of the States are done away, and their expenses come to be limited within their natural compass, the possibility almost of interference (of state revenue laws with federal ones) will vanish.

36. Taxation

Who will argue that federal taxation is not "really inconvenient?"

XXXVI. CONCERNING THE GENERAL POWER OF TAXATION

(It will be) a fixed point of policy in the national administration to go as far as may be practicable in making the luxury of the rich tributary to the public treasury, in order to diminish the necessity of those impositions which might create dissatisfaction in the poorer and most numerous classes of the society.

36. Taxation

It was anticipated that all or virtually all citizens would contribute to the welfare of the federal government, paying taxes in some form or other. In Europe there had been various mechanisms by which the wealthy were able to avoid paying taxes altogether while taxation of the poor rose proportionally, checked only by their extinction, emigration, or rebellion. (See Charles Adams, *For Good and Evil*, 1993.) It was intended that the rich should pay to support the government and that taxes on poorer individuals should be less. It was not intended that taxation of the former should be increased to the point of their extinction, emigration, or rebellion.

XXXVII. CONCERNING THE DIFFICULTIES OF THE CONVENTION IN DEVISING A PROPER FORM OF GOVERNMENT

Stability in government is essential to national character and to the advantages annexed to it, as well as to that repose and confidence in the minds of the people, which are among the chief blessings of civil society. An irregular and mutable legislation is not more an evil in itself than it is odious to the people.

37. Excessive Legislation

Americans always have been known as faddish, but changeability and change for its own sake have been carried to the level of fetish in recent years. This is reflected in the quantity of regulation as represented by the number of pages in THE FEDERAL REGISTER, going from 2,620 pages in 1936 to an astonishing 78,961 pages in 2012. Since 1993 it has averaged 71,470 pages per year. The income tax regulations alone run to nearly 75,000 pages (increased from 400 pages in 1913 when the income tax became law). Who reads all that stuff? "Change" is a regular theme and promise of presidential candidates; the nature of that change is never entirely clear, and never actually results in a decrease in the sheer quantity of law-making. Madison was quite clear about the importance of stable, unchanging government.

XXXVII. CONCERNING THE DIFFICULTIES OF THE CONVENTION IN DEVISING A PROPER FORM OF GOVERNMENT

The genius of republican liberty seems to demand on one side, not only that all power should be derived from the people, but that those entrusted with it should be kept in dependence on the people, by a short duration of their appointment; and that even during this short period the trust should be placed not in a few, but a number of hands.

37. Term Limits

The need for "short duration" of service in an elected capacity resulted in the terms of the members of the House of Representatives being limited to two years. But in our day gerrymandered districts, special interest donations, large staffs, and other incumbent advantages and political tricks have resulted in terms lasting two years times ten, fifteen, twenty, or more.

Officials serving under such conditions become ever more estranged from the people and from the nature and quality of life under the laws they have passed.

XXXIX. THE CONFORMITY OF THE PLAN TO REPUBLICAN PRINCIPLES

In this relation, then, the proposed government cannot be deemed a *national* one; since its jurisdiction extends to certain enumerated objects only, and leaves to the several States a residuary and inviolable sovereignty over all other objects.

39. Limited Government

The importance of this principle cannot be overstressed, that American government is intended to be limited. It is not meant to become a substitute nanny for citizens; the welfare state that grew up in the twentieth century is frankly foreign to the American tradition (and to be distinguished from charity, always widespread and readily available in this country but administered by individuals, churches, other private institutions, and local governments). The authority of the federal government is limited only to those specific areas mentioned in the Constitution and activity beyond those areas is a usurpation of liberty. So important is this concept that it was explicitly added to Constitution in the form of the Tenth Amendment, now largely forgotten, ignored, and disregarded. It is unlikely that the federal behemoth can be reformed from within--the people must demand that the states reassert their rights under the Tenth Amendment.

XLIII. THE POWERS CONFERRED BY THE CONSTITUTION FURTHER CONSIDERED

But as new-fangled and artificial treasons have been the great engines by which violent factions, the natural offspring of free government, have usually wreaked their alternate malignity on each other, the convention have, with great judgment, opposed a barrier to this peculiar danger, by inserting a constitutional definition of the crime . . .

43. Independent Agencies and Judicial Corruption

While not yet elevated to the level of treason, the recent creation of a host of "environmental" crimes under which property can be taken and even prison terms imposed by agencies without jury trial and only limited judicial review are just as offensive to our traditional sense of what constitutes tyranny. Search and seizure committed by independent agencies under RICO, the Patriot Act, and other overly general statutes likewise belong in this category. And what of the destruction of the Branch

Davidians in Waco, Texas; did the Davidians' "offense" perhaps represent a new definition of treason in the eyes of the BATF?

XLIV. RESTRICTIONS ON THE AUTHORITY OF THE SEVERAL STATES

Bills of attainder, *ex-post-facto* laws, and laws impairing the obligation of contracts, are contrary to the first principles of the social compact, and to every principle of sound legislation. The two former are expressly prohibited by the declarations prefixed to some of the State constitutions, and all of them are prohibited by the spirit and scope of these fundamental charters. Our own experience has taught us, nevertheless, that additional fences against these dangers ought not to be omitted. Very properly, therefore, have the convention added this constitutional bulwark in favor of personal security and private rights . . .

44. Limited Government

Contrary to the opinion of the Supreme Court at the time, the imposition by Congress and the Clinton administration of taxes, including estate taxes, with their accompanying manifold regulations retroactively to before they were even in office is the very definition of an *ex-post-facto* law. That retroactivity was sustained by the Court is further testimony to the critical condition of our constitutional system--the third branch cannot be depended upon to consistently restrain the other two. As for impairing the obligation of contracts, a host of regulations in financial and other areas have done just this. One thinks notably of regulations prohibiting physicians from contracting with Medicare patients for payment of their bills even when the patients are financially willing and able to do so. Doctors are threatened with charges of fraud (punishable by exorbitant fines and jail terms) for so much as accidental billing of patients for unpaid balances. The inadequacy of Medicare reimbursements results in the balance of the costs being shifted to private-pay and other patients not bound by Medicare rules.

XLIV. RESTRICTIONS ON THE AUTHORITY OF THE SEVERAL STATES

If it be asked what is to be the consequence, in case the Congress shall misconstrue this part of the Constitution, and exercise powers not warranted by its true meaning, I answer, . . . the success of the usurpation will depend on the executive and judiciary departments, which are to expound and give effect to the legislative acts; and in the last resort a remedy must be obtained from the people, who can, by the election of more faithful representatives, annul the acts of the usurpers.

44. Government Corruption: Reelect? De-elect!

This is, of course, the ultimate peaceful answer to the problems of modern government, namely elective action by the people to put in office "more faithful representatives." When the Supreme Court ruled a few years ago in support of Roe v. Wade, Representative Shirley Chisholm said, "The Supreme Court has spoken and that is the end of the matter." She could not have been more wrong. Ultimate power in a democratic system does not rest with unelected judges, nor even with the legislature, though they are the official representatives of the people: ultimate power rests with the people themselves.

Particularly on an issue of great moral significance to large portions of the population, a legal pronouncement by one Supreme Court at one moment in time cannot be the "end of the matter." Liberal jurists taking extreme positions on the modern Court play at most a delaying action on abortion, much as Southern jurists did on the antebellum Court with slavery. Successful, long-term national policy must be a true reflection of the hearts of the people.

So, too, with the larger question of the entire monstrosity of modern federal bureaucracy--the welfare state and its pestilential regulations. It must be replaced with a much smaller and more efficient government which conforms to the spirit and letter of the Constitution. Court cases on this particular issue or that are one thing, but in the end true reform must be accomplished by electing representatives who will be faithful to the Constitution as well as by appointing new judges who will be similarly scrupulous. To this end the people generally must be awakened, awakened to a sense of the awful danger that looms if such changes are not effected.

XLV. THE ALLEGED DANGER FROM THE POWERS OF THE UNION TO THE STATE GOVERNMENTS CONSIDERED

The powers delegated by the proposed Constitution to the federal government are few and defined. Those which are to remain in the State governments are numerous and indefinite. The former will be exercised principally on external objects, as war, peace, negotiation, and foreign commerce; with the last the power of taxation will, for the most part, be connected. The powers reserved to the several States will extend to all the objects which, in the ordinary course of affairs; concern the lives, liberties, and properties of the people, and the internal order, improvement, and prosperity of the State.

The operations of the federal government will be most extensive and important in times of war and danger; those of the State governments in times of peace and security. As the former periods will bear a small proportion to the latter, the State governments will here enjoy another advantage over the federal government. The more adequate, indeed, the federal powers may be rendered to the national defence, the less frequent will be those scenes of danger which might favor their ascendancy over the governments of the particular States.

45. Limited Government

Here again the promise is made and the plan made explicit that the federal government is to be limited primarily to matters of foreign policy, with the individual states responsible for domestic affairs. This division of responsibility was based on very practical principles, namely, that foreign matters are of necessity a concern of the general government while that same government is too removed from the people to be adequate or adequately controlled in everyday life. Furthermore, it was recognized that different locales with their variations in culture must of necessity and by preference deal with domestic matters in somewhat different ways. It may be argued that the homogenization of the country since the introduction of highways, telephone, television and internet has eliminated regional variation. This is only half true. A national culture has arisen, but it is accompanied by an even greater appreciation for those state and local differences that survive, thus increasing their importance. Homogenization to the point of lock-step, Brave New World uniformity is antithetical to the American spirit.

XLVI. THE INFLUENCE OF THE STATE AND FEDERAL GOVERNMENTS COMPARED

(T)he first and most natural attachment of the people will be to the governments of their respective States . . . By the superintending care of these, all the more domestic and personal interests of the people will be regulated and provided for . . .

If . . . the people should in future become more partial to the federal than to the State governments, the change can only result from such manifest and irresistible proofs of a better administration, as will overcome all their antecedent propensities. And in that case, the people ought not surely to be precluded from giving most of their confidence where they may discover it to be most due; but even in that case the State governments could have little to apprehend, because it is only within a certain sphere that the federal power can, in the nature of things, be advantageously administered.

46. States' Rights

So even if the federal government is loved by the people, it could not encroach upon the states because a central government is not capable of being "advantageously administered" beyond certain limited matters, namely those areas specified in the Constitution. We now have ample proof of these words all around us in wasteful and counterproductive programs which have, in a sort of agonizing national experiment, gone far beyond that "certain sphere" of proper federal power. Take, for instance, the War on Poverty. Dramatic increases in costs since 1965 have nevertheless seen little change in the percentage of Americans living in poverty as defined by the census, with actual increases in poverty rate and absolute numbers in recent years. Similar observations can be made in education with the disastrous "no child left behind" and Common Core programs or in health care with Medicare, Medicaid, and Obamacare. The greatest improvements in all these areas occurred prior to the creation of federal programs.

XLVI. THE INFLUENCE OF THE STATE AND FEDERAL GOVERNMENTS COMPARED

(If the federal army should be used to oppress the people) the State governments, with the people on their side, would be able to repel the danger . . . To these (federal troops) would be opposed a militia amounting to near half a million of citizens with arms in their hands, officered by men chosen from among themselves, fighting for their common liberties, and united and conducted by governments possessing their affections and confidence . . . (It is) the advantage of being armed, which the Americans possess over the people of almost every other nation . . .

46. Gun Control

Here again, the founding fathers are clear that the right of the people to bear arms is not so that they can get their own food or enjoy target practice, but so that they can defend themselves against oppression. The potential source of that oppression is their own government. The National Rifle Association correctly points out how the National Socialists in Germany first registered all the weapons in the country, then confiscated them. Aside from its unconstitutionality, increased gun control also risks further decreasing the respect of law-abiding citizens for their government, for as regulations increase, more and more ordinary people choose not to obey them.

Indeed, if private arms were prohibited and confiscated, it is likely that millions of Americans simply would not comply. They would become technical criminals, while real criminals would remain unaffected. Interesting to note, our highest murder and other crime rates are in cities with the strictest gun control laws such as Chicago, Washington D. C., Los Angeles, Baltimore, New

York City, and so forth. The inverse relationship between armed citizens and violent crime was well documented by John R. Lott, Jr. in his 1998 book, *More Guns, Less Crime*.

XLVII. THE PARTICULAR STRUCTURE OF THE NEW GOVERNMENT AND THE DISTRIBUTION OF POWER AMONG ITS DIFFERENT PARTS

The accumulation of all powers, legislative, executive, and judiciary, in the same hands, whether of one, a few, or many, and whether hereditary, self-appointed, or elective, may justly be pronounced the very definition of tyranny.

47. Independent Agencies

Notice in this very important definition that tyranny may exist in an elected system with many representatives as well as in other forms of government. The key is the presence of all three powers in one institution. One immediately thinks of the various independent agencies created over the past century--the Internal Revenue Service, the Food and Drug Administration, the Environmental Protection Agency, the Occupational Safety and Health Administration, the Equal Employment Opportunity Commission, and so forth. These agencies have power, based on only tenuous Congressional guidelines, to create specific regulations, enforce obedience to those regulations, and levy fines and confiscate property when they deem the regulations to have been broken. Appeal from their decisions is difficult, expensive, and sometimes not possible at all. Madison himself provides the descriptive noun for such institutions. Power they have; moral authority is another matter.

XLVIII. THESE DEPARTMENTS SHOULD NOT BE SO FAR SEPARATED AS TO HAVE NO CONSTITUTIONAL CONTROL OVER EACH OTHER

The legislative department is everywhere extending the sphere of its activity, and drawing all power into its impetuous vortex.

The founders of our republics (the states) have so much merit for the wisdom which they have displayed, that no task can be less pleasing than that of pointing out the errors into which they have fallen . . . They seem never to have recollected the danger from legislative usurpations, which, by assembling all power in the same hands, must lead to the same tyranny as is threatened by executive usurpations . . .

(I)t is against the enterprising ambition of this department that the people ought to indulge all their jealousy and exhaust all their precautions . . .

(I)t can, with the greater facility, mask, under complicated and indirect measures, the encroachments which it makes on the coordinate departments . . .

It will be no alleviation, that these powers will be exercised by a plurality of hands, and not by a single one. One hundred and seventy-three despots would surely be as oppressive as one . . . As little will it avail us, that they are chosen by ourselves. An *elective despotism* was not the government we fought for; but one which should not only be founded on free principles, but in which the powers of governments should be so divided and balanced among several bodies of magistracy, as that no one could transcend their legal limits, without being effectually checked and restrained by the others.

48. Limited Government and the Imperial Congress

The authors of the Constitution had ample experience not only from history and foreign governments about the danger of excess power, but also first-hand experience with the various colonial and state governments. The legislatures had shown themselves quite as able to abuse their power as any monarch. This continues to be the case in our day.

XLIX. METHOD OF GUARDING AGAINST THE ENCROACHMENTS OF ANY ONE DEPARTMENT OF GOVERNMENT BY APPEALING TO THE PEOPLE THROUGH A CONVENTION

(A)s every appeal to the people would carry an implication of some defect in the government, frequent appeals would, in a great measure, deprive the government of that veneration which time bestows on everything, and without which perhaps the wisest and freest governments would not possess the requisite stability . . .

The danger of disturbing the public tranquillity by interesting too strongly the public passions, is a still more serious objection against frequent reference of constitutional questions to the decision of the whole society.

49. Excessive Legislation

In the age of cell phones and faxes, internet and cable news, Facebook and Twitter, with national and international news bombarding us constantly through the 24 hour news cycle, it may be quaint to recall that preserving "public tranquillity" is one of the very important purposes of government. We have come so far from this principle that whole presidential campaigns can be based on the notion of change without regard for what that change might be. Some candidates have promoted creation of an electronic town-meeting system, not primarily for the commendable purpose of open debate and discussion, but rather as a foundation for frequent national referenda--government by polling. This could create something approaching national democracy, a system that would further undermine the principle of representation embedded in the Constitution.

This quote specifically has to do with matters of constitutional amendment. It is a mistake of some modern activists to suppose that by turning their particular issue into an amendment (whether it be a balanced budget, freedom of or freedom from abortion, equal rights, or any of a number of issues) they can thus decrease the likelihood that a victory in the legislature this year may be overturned by their opponents next year. But the stability of the system as a whole is more important than any of these individual issues; satisfactory, lasting resolution of such issues depends on continual attention to the structure, behavior, and composition of the representative body, not tinkering with the fundamental law itself.

LI. THE STRUCTURE OF A GOVERNMENT MUST FURNISH THE PROPER CHECKS AND BALANCES BETWEEN THE DIFFERENT DEPARTMENTS

In a free government the security for civil rights must be the same as that for religious rights. It consists in the one case in the multiplicity of interests, and in the other in the multiplicity of sects . . . Justice is the end of government. It is the end of civil society. It ever has been and ever will be pursued until it be obtained, or until liberty be lost in the pursuit.

51. Justice

The concern here is with the danger of majority rule and the preservation of minority rights. It is interesting that the author presupposed little difficulty in preserving freedom of religion, using it for the comparative example in discussing civil rights. The existence of so many denominations causes them all to have an interest in preserving their mutual freedom. Similarly with civil rights in general, they are preserved by "many parts, interests, and classes of citizens."

LII. THE HOUSE OF REPRESENTATIVES

(I)t is particularly essential that the branch of it under consideration (the House of Representatives) should have an immediate dependence on, and an intimate sympathy with, the people. Frequent elections are unquestionably the only policy by which this dependence and sympathy can be effectually secured.

52. Term Limits

Hence the two-year term for House members, compared with six for senators. But "safe seats", moneyed special interests, and incumbent advantage have eroded the effectiveness of short terms in keeping congressmen in "intimate sympathy" with the people; it is time to limit the number of terms as well as their individual length. A universal provision for recall elections could also be a useful tool.

LIII. THE HOUSE OF REPRESENTATIVES

The most laborious task will be the proper inauguration of the government and the primeval formation of a federal code. Improvements on the first draughts will every year become both easier and fewer. Past transactions of the government will be a ready and accurate source of information to new members.

53. Excessive Legislation

It was expected after the first few years that the number and complexity of new laws would decrease. After all, once the law is written it does not have to be written again, except for occasional clarifications and elaborations as circumstances dictate, right? Alas, this has not been the case within living memory. Each year there are hundreds of new laws and thousands of new regulations. The government printing office produces thousands of pages, providing much work for bureaucrats, lawyers, and accountants but very little understanding for the ordinary citizen.

The health care law commonly called Obamacare runs to over 20,000 pages, was written in secret, and passed by party line vote. Which of our elected officials actually reads the legislation they vote on? Laws which are so numerous, so lengthy, and so complex that even experienced lawyers cannot understand them do not deserve the respect and reverence of the people, and are not in keeping with the vision of constitutional law promised to us by our ancestors.

LV. THE TOTAL NUMBER OF THE HOUSE OF REPRESENTATIVES

I am unable to conceive that the people of America, in their present temper, or under any circumstances which can speedily happen, will choose, and every second year repeat the choice of, sixty-five or one hundred men who would be disposed to form and pursue a scheme of tyranny or treachery . . . What change of circumstances, time, and a fuller population of our country may produce, requires a prophetic spirit to declare, which makes no part of my pretensions.

55. Corruption

We now have the "prophetic spirit" of history to help us more readily envision those circumstances.

LV. THE TOTAL NUMBER OF THE HOUSE OF REPRESENTATIVES

As there is a degree of depravity in mankind which requires a certain degree of circumspection and distrust, so there are other qualities in human nature which justify a certain portion of esteem and confidence. Republican government presupposes the existence of these qualities in a higher degree than any other form.

55. Character

Put another way, representative government requires public virtue, and while that public virtue is not identical with private virtue it is related to it. Character matters. It matters not only in candidates for public office, but in the citizens who vote for them. Alexis de Tocqueville wrote, "I sought for the greatness and genius of America in her commodious harbors and her ample rivers, and it was not there; in her fertile fields and boundless prairies, and it was not there; in her rich mines and her vast world of commerce, and it was not there. Not until I went to the churches of America and heard her pulpits aflame with righteousness did I understand the secret of her genius and power. America is great because she is good and if America ever ceases to be good, America will cease to be great."

LVI. THE TOTAL NUMBER OF THE HOUSE OF REPRESENTATIVES

What are to be the objects of federal legislation? Those which are of most importance, and which seem most to require local knowledge, are commerce, taxation, and the militia . . .

Taxation will consist, in a great measure, of duties which will be involved in the regulation of commerce . . . In every State there have been made, and must continue to be made, regulations on this subject which will, in many cases, leave little more to be done by the federal legislature, than to review the different laws, and reduce them in one general act.

56. Limited Government

In the context of eighteenth century mercantilism, a system of tariffs, posts, and excises was a rational source of revenue. It no longer makes sense in the age of free trade. The two important points in this quotation are that taxation was not intended to be directly upon the people and that federal regulations were intended to be for simplification and unification. Each state is a separate experiment in self-government; the principles learned in those experiments and the laws derived from them are to be the building blocks of the federal code.

LVII. THE ALLEGED TENDENCY OF THE NEW PLAN TO ELEVATE THE FEW AT THE EXPENSE OF THE MANY CONSIDERED IN CONNECTION WITH REPRESENTATION

The aim of every political constitution is, or ought to be, first to obtain for rulers men who possess most wisdom to discern, and most virtue to pursue, the common good of the society; and in the next place, to take the most effectual precautions for keeping them virtuous whilst they continue to hold their public trust. The elective mode of obtaining rulers is the characteristic policy of republican government. The means relied on in this form of government for preventing their degeneracy are numerous and various. The most effectual one, is such a limitation of the term of appointments as will maintain a proper responsibility to the people . . .

(T)he House of Representatives is so constituted as to support in the members an habitual recollection of their dependence on the people.

57. Term Limits

The 1992 elections resulted in an unprecedented number of freshman legislators who had committed themselves to dramatic reform of the government; similar sweeping changes of personnel occurred in 2010 and 2012. Those commitments were soon crushed by the realities of entrenched power based on a seniority system that kept power not so much in the hands of one party as of one political type--the corrupt professional political hack of both parties. The precautions created by the founders for "keeping them virtuous" while in office were more or less effective for the first 150 years of the union, but now have become inadequate. Term limitations in 1788 meant election for only two, four, or six years at a time. It is now time to extend the principle to the number of times that election can occur, thus requiring even closer accountability of elected officials.

LVII. THE ALLEGED TENDENCY OF THE NEW PLAN TO ELEVATE THE FEW AT THE EXPENSE OF THE MANY CONSIDERED IN CONNECTION WITH REPRESENTATION

I will add, as a fifth circumstance in the situation of the House of Representatives, restraining them from oppressive measures, that they can make no law which will not have its full operation on themselves and their friends, as well as on the great mass of the society. This has always been deemed one of the strongest bonds by which human policy can connect the rulers and the people together. . .

If it be asked, what is to restrain the House of Representatives from making legal discriminations in favor of themselves and a particular class of the society? I answer: the genius of the whole system; the nature of just and constitutional laws; and above all, the vigilant and manly spirit which actuates the people of America--a spirit which nourishes freedom, and in return is nourished by it.

If this spirit shall ever be so far debased as to tolerate a law not obligatory on the legislature, as well as on the people, the people will be prepared to tolerate anything but liberty.

57. The Imperial Congress

That Congress routinely exempts itself from the laws it passes has become a national humiliation. Such laws include the Social Security Act, the Civil Rights Act, the Americans With Disabilities Act, the Age Discrimination in Employment Act, the National Labor Relations Act, the Occupational Safety and Health Act, the Equal Pay Act, the Family and Medical Leave Act, the Patient Protection and Affordable Care Act (Obamacare), and more. Thus Congress has severed one of the "strongest bonds" that can bind it to the people; thus congressional arrogance has made that "world's greatest deliberative body" an object of contempt in the eyes of its citizens.

LVIII. OBJECTION THAT THE NUMBER OF MEMBERS WILL NOT BE AUGMENTED AS THE PROGRESS OF POPULATION

This power over the purse may, in fact, be regarded as the most complete and effectual weapon with which any constitution can arm the immediate representatives of the people, for obtaining a redress of every grievance, and for carrying into effect every just and salutary measure . . .

In the first place, the more numerous an assembly may be, of whatever characters composed, the greater is known to be the ascendancy of passion over reason. In the next place, the larger the number, the greater will be the proportion of members of limited information and weak capacities. Now, it is precisely on characters of this description that the eloquence and address of the few are known to act with all their force. In the ancient republics, where the whole body of the people assembled in person, a single orator, or an artful statesman, was generally seen to rule with as complete a sway as if a sceptre had been placed in his single hand. On the same principle, the more multitudinous a representative assembly may be rendered, the more it will partake of the infirmities incident to collective meetings of the people. Ignorance will be the dupe of cunning and passion the slave of sophistry and declamation. The people can never err more than in supposing that by multiplying their representatives beyond a certain limit, they strengthen the barrier against government of a few. Experience will forever admonish them that, on the contrary, *after securing a sufficient number for the purposes of safety of local information, and of diffusive sympathy with the whole society,* they will counteract their own views by every addition to their representatives. The countenance of the government may become more democratic, but the soul that animates it will be more oligarchic. The machine will be enlarged, but the fewer, and often the more secret, will be the springs by which its motions are directed.

58. Democracy

These arguments originally were applied to

the error of making the legislature too large, by causing it to approximate democracy rather than republicanism. But today, the same arguments apply with equal validity to the error of excessive referenda, over-reliance on polls as guidance for decision making, and the mistaken notion that national "town meetings" can replace congressional deliberation and debate. That government actions now tend toward greater secrecy was exemplified by the secret, indeed, illegal meetings of the Health Care Task Force during the Clinton administration, the secret and widespread power of the National Security Agency, and ever increased secrecy throughout the federal government under Obama.

LVIII. OBJECTION THAT THE NUMBER OF MEMBERS WILL NOT BE AUGMENTED AS THE PROGRESS OF POPULATION

(In settings requiring a super-majority) power would be transferred to the minority . . . an interested minority might take advantage of it to screen themselves from equitable sacrifice to the general weal, or, in particular emergencies, to extort unreasonable indulgences.

58. Partisanship and Democracy

The problem described here is seen regularly in parliamentary systems such as Israel, Italy, or

Britain in which the government is created by a coalition of parties. It is often the minor party, sometimes from the political fringe, that makes the difference between success and failure, thus exercising disproportionate power. Lack of strong third party organizations makes this less common in America, but ad-hoc groups with special interests either within or without one of the major parties, still demand concessions when votes are close, a routine occurrence in divided governments. Practice governing a small, corrupt, one-party state did not prepare President Bill Clinton to seek broad, bipartisan consensus on issues; it was only the loss of control of Congress in 1994 that forced him into compromise. Similarly, President Obama, with no executive and only limited legislative experience, is a rigid ideologue who regularly demonizes his opponents, refuses to include them in discussions, and does not understand or accept the principles of negotiation and compromise in the governing process. More "normal" times would see these degrees of extremist influence only during veto overrides or votes on constitutional amendments, as suggested in the above excerpt.

LXI. CONCERNING THE POWER OF CONGRESS TO REGULATE THE ELECTION OF MEMBERS

If an improper spirit of any kind should happen to prevail in it (the House of Representatives), that spirit would be apt to infuse itself into the new members, as they come forward in succession. The mass would be likely to remain nearly the same, assimilating constantly to itself its gradual accretions. There is a contagion in example which few men have sufficient force of mind to resist. I am inclined to think that treble the duration of office, with the condition of a total dissolution of the body at the same time might be less formidable to liberty than one-third of that duration subject to gradual and successive alterations.

Uniformity in the time of elections seems not less requisite for executing the idea of a regular rotation in the Senate, and for conveniently assembling the legislature as a stated period in each year.

61. Term Limits

Hamilton anticipated in this passage that the House of Representatives would be completely reorganized and reconstituted with each election, thus maintaining a close relationship between the representatives and the people and eliminating any "improper spirit" that might be in the House. Our current system does not accomplish this, however, with House seats converted into individual fiefdoms in perpetuity. It is as if a sign were posted on the Capital doors, "no outsider need apply."

LXII. THE SENATE

(T)he facility and excess of law-making seem to be the diseases to which our governments are most liable . . .

62. Excessive Legislation

This is still the case.

LXII. THE SENATE

What indeed are all the repealing, explaining, and amending laws, which fill and disgrace our voluminous codes, but so many monuments of deficient wisdom; so many impeachments exhibited by each succeeding against each preceding session; so many admonitions to the people, of the value of those aids which may be expected from a well-constituted Senate?

A good government implies two things: first, fidelity to the object of government, which is the happiness of the people; secondly, a knowledge of the means by which that object can be best attained. Some governments are deficient in both these qualities; most governments are deficient in the first. I scruple to assert, that in American governments too little attention has been paid to the last. . .

The internal effects of a mutable policy are still more calamitous. It poisons the blessings of liberty itself. It will be of little avail to the people, that the laws are made by men of their own choice, if the laws be so voluminous that they cannot be read, or so incoherent that they cannot be understood; if they be repealed or revised before they are promulgated, or undergo such incessant changes that no man, who knows what the law is to-day can guess what it will be tomorrow. Law is defined to be a rule of action; but how can that be a rule, which is little known, and less fixed?

62. Excessive Legislation

It was expected that the Senate would prevent the House from continually changing and adding to federal laws. Considering how bad it might have been, we may suppose that this objective was at least partly accomplished; certainly large quantities of proposed legislation die each year between houses. And yet, each year's crop of new laws is still greater than ever and the regulations (written by unelected, anonymous bureaucrats) are so extensive that no sensible citizen would bother reading them. And inasmuch as the laws are constantly changing, the respect of the average citizen for those laws and for the lawmakers is further diminished.

LXII. THE SENATE

Another effect of public instability is the unreasonable advantage it gives to the sagacious, the enterprising, and the moneyed few over the industrious and uninformed mass of the people. Every new regulation concerning commerce or revenue, or in any manner affecting the value of the different species of property, presents a new harvest to those who watch the change, and can trace its consequences; a harvest, reared not by themselves, but the the toils and cares of the great body of their fellow-citizens. This is a state of things in which it may be said with some truth that laws are made for the *few*, not for the *many*.

In another point of view, great injury results from an unstable government. The want of confidence in the public councils damps every useful undertaking, the success and profit of which may depend on a continuance of existing arrangements . . .

But the most deplorable effect of all is that diminution of attachment and reverence which steals into the hearts of the people, towards a political system which betrays so many marks of infirmity, and disappoints so many of their flattering hopes. No government, any more than an individual, will long be respected without being truly respectable; nor be truly respectable, without possessing a certain portion of order and stability.

62. Excessive Regulation and Corruption

It is neither unexpected nor unreasonable that many wealthy, ambitious individuals maintain close relationships with party leaders and government officials. Companies, unions, and other organizations hire armies of well-paid lobbyists not to look after the interests of the citizenry, but to look for the twists and turns of law buried in the avalanche of words created by every legislature that will give them some relative advantage in business or investment, and to insert a paragraph here and a provision there which will give them special privileges. Their investment in politics is more than repaid. And so the average citizen's cynicism grows while confidence in politicians and the political system withers.

LXIII. THE SENATE

(L)iberty may be endangered by the abuses of liberty as well as by the abuses of power . . . there are numerous instances of the former as well as of the latter; and . . . the former rather than the latter, are apparently most to be apprehended by the United States.

LXIV. THE POWER OF THE SENATE

This mode (of election by state-designated electors) has, in such cases, vastly the advantage of elections by the people in their collective capacity, where the activity of party zeal, taking advantage of the supineness, the ignorance, and the hopes and fears of the unwary and interested, often places men in office by the votes of a small proportion of the electors.

63 and 64. Democracy

This fault of general elections is particularly evident in close elections with low voter turnout, resulting in office-holders who are actually elected by small minorities of the population. This is not to say that huge voter turnout is desirable. Quite the contrary; citizens should vote only if they are informed and capable of making wise decisions. Excessive amounts of media misinformation as well as party propaganda make the creation of an informed electorate in our age difficult, perhaps because of rather than in spite of superior modern communications. This is made even worse by the rise of certain politicians who not only stretch the truth or manipulate statistics, but say bald-faced lies without apparent repercussion. But the solution is not more regulation, restriction, and censorship, but more freedom, ethical and unbiased reporting, and truthful education.

These quotations refer to selection of senators by state governments, rather than direct election. The reason for this was to enhance the power of the states over the federal government, ensure that senators would represent the interests of the states and their respective governments, and increase the likelihood that only highly qualified individuals would be selected. This mechanism was destroyed with the passage of the Seventeenth Amendment in 1913 which required direct election of senators by the people, thus making them subject to all the political winds and intrigues as members of the House.

LXVIII. THE MODE OF ELECTING THE PRESIDENT

It was also peculiarly desirable to afford as little opportunity as possible to tumult and disorder . . . And as the electors, chosen in each State, are to assemble and vote in the State in which they are chosen, this detached and divided situation will expose them much less to heats and ferments, which might be communicated from them to the people, than if they were all to be convened at one time, in one place.

68. Campaign Reform

The electoral system today is much different from the one argued for in THE FEDERALIST, but the principle of avoiding "heats and ferments" is still a good one. Issues of national importance should not be decided by the passion of the moment or during a time of enthusiastic zeal. Avoidance of such situations is one reason power in our republican system was divided and separated, so the "heat and ferment" of one party or branch is less likely to spill over to the others and bring down the whole structure.

LXVIII. THE MODE OF ELECTING THE PRESIDENT

The process of election affords a moral certainty, that the office of President will never fall to the lot of any man who is not in an eminent degree endowed with the requisite qualifications. Talents for low intrigue, and the little arts of popularity, may alone suffice to elevate a man to the first honors in a single State; but it will require other talents, and a different merit, to establish him in the esteem and confidence of the whole Union, or of so considerable a portion of it as would be necessary to make him a successful candidate for the distinguished office of President of the United States. It will not be too strong to say, that there will be a constant probability of seeing the station filled by characters preeminent for ability and virtue.

68. Presidential virtue

The author was right, by and large, for the greater part of two centuries. Perhaps the recent and current exceptions prove the rule.

LXX. THE EXECUTIVE DEPARTMENT FURTHER CONSIDERED

The ingredients which constitute safety in the republican sense are, first, a due dependence on the people; secondly, a due responsibility.

70. Term Limits

The importance of "due dependence on the people" has been mentioned before in the context of term limitation. "Due responsibility" is another matter. Politicians in our day have developed to a high degree their ability to avoid responsibility. Nowhere is this more evident than in the passage of laws indexing future increases of salaries, benefits, or "entitlement." This establishes a system in which future votes are unnecessary and past deeds can be forgotten while the benefits of those deeds go on unchecked. An even more egregious evasion of accountability to the point of frank dishonesty has been the practice of the "discharge petition", under which congressmen tell their constituents that they were in favor of a measure while secretly withholding their votes to let it out of committee. Such contemptible behavior, when revealed, further diminishes the public honor which otherwise would be accorded Congress. Of course, these principles apply as well to the Executive as to the Legislature.

LXX. THE EXECUTIVE DEPARTMENT FURTHER CONSIDERED

Men often oppose a thing, merely because they have had no agency in planning it, or because it may have been planned by those whom they dislike. But if they have been consulted, and have happened to disapprove, opposition then becomes, in their estimation, an indispensable duty of self-love . . .

In the legislature, promptitude of decision is oftener an evil than a benefit. The differences of opinion, and the jarrings of parties in that department of the government, though they may sometimes obstruct salutary plans, yet often promotes deliberation and circumspection, and serve to check excesses in the majority . . . But no favorable circumstances palliate or atone for the disadvantages of dissension in the executive department.

70. Avoiding Haste

The often agonizing pace of the legislative process is a source of frustration to the public as well as to members of government, especially now in the electronic age of short attention spans. But slowness and apparent inefficiency are intentional to prevent or at least decrease the incidence of error. (A case in point is the haste in the debate over health care reform, giving us the spectacle of legislators voting for a monstrosity of legislation they had not, and could not have read, and of a Speaker, Nancy Pelosi, who said they had to "pass it to find out what is in it.") This glacial pace in Congress is balanced by the relative strength and potential alacrity of the executive branch. That ability to act promptly and resolutely is compromised if members of the executive branch are in significant open disagreement. Again, however, the recent examples of executive agencies and the president himself acting rashly, unilaterally, beyond their constitutionally defined authority, and against the will of the people and their representatives, are—one hopes—notable exceptions.

LXXI. THE DURATION IN OFFICE OF THE EXECUTIVE

The tendency of the legislative authority to absorb every other, has been fully displayed and illustrated . . . The representatives of the people, in a popular assembly, seem sometimes to fancy that they are the people themselves, and betray strong symptoms of impatience and disgust at the least sign of opposition from any other quarter; as if the exercise of its rights, by either the executive or judiciary, were a breach of their privilege and an outrage to their dignity. They often appear disposed to exert an imperious control over the other departments . . .

(T)he best security for the fidelity of mankind is to make their interest coincide with their duty.

71. Arrogance, the Imperial Congress, and the Imperial President

Congress has been particularly aggressive in expanding its power relative to the presidency following periods of presidential embarrassment such as after Watergate, during much of the Carter administration, and during the latter portions of the Reagan and first Bush administrations. This took on a partisan character because of long-lasting, one-party rule in the legislature. How then to explain the lack of congressional assertion of power during the remarkably expansive and repeatedly illegal actions of the Obama years? When controlled by the same party, they presumably agreed with him, but when controlled by the opposing party, why are there no concrete actions, special prosecutors, indictments, etc.? Does an unprecedentedly arrogant, Imperial President intimidate them? Or has Congress become so corrupt they simply want to stay at the trough and not "rock the boat"? Do their personal interests coincide with their duty?

LXXIII. THE PROVISION FOR THE SUPPORT OF THE EXECUTIVE AND THE VETO POWER

It may perhaps be said that the power of preventing bad laws (by veto) includes that of preventing good ones; and may be used to the one purpose as well as to the other. But this objection will have little weight with those who can properly estimate the mischief of that inconstancy and mutability in the laws, which form the greatest blemish in the character and genius of our governments. They will consider every institution calculated to restrain the excess of law-making, and to keep things in the same state at which they happen to be at any given period, as much more likely to do good than harm; because it is favorable to greater stability in the system of legislation. The injury which may possibly be done by defeating a few good laws, will be amply compensated by the advantage of preventing a number of bad ones.

73. Excessive Legislation

Here again we recall the importance of stability in government, the constant changing of laws being called the "greatest blemish" of our government. We have already observed how an "excess of lawmaking" has become characteristic of modern American government. This increased complexity of the law combines with increased bureaucracy to provide incumbents with one of their key advantages over challengers—constituent services. Legislators now spend large portions of their time and employ numerous staff members (at public expense) responding to individual citizen requests for help in navigating the federal maze. Laws are so complex that only the legislative assistants who actually wrote them can tell what they mean or how to satisfy their demands!

LXXIII. THE PROVISION FOR THE SUPPORT OF THE EXECUTIVE AND THE VETO POWER

It is impossible to keep the judges too distinct from every other avocation than that of expounding the laws. It is peculiarly dangerous to place them in a situation to be either corrupted or influenced by the Executive.

73. Justice

A more circuitous form of "influence" occurred under the Clinton administration, with the unprecedented discharge of U.S. attorneys, their replacement in some instances with cronies of the president, and alleged limitation of investigations by prosecutors and regulatory agencies, most notably in financial matters. Rather than run the risk of tampering with judges directly, it is now easier just to prevent embarrassing and possibly illegal activities from ever coming to court in the first place. Or in the case of the Obama "Justice" Department, bringing or not bringing cases according to a strict, extreme ideology rather than according to established principles of law and equal justice. Never has the undue influence of the Executive on the Justice Department been so flagrant. President Obama's first Attorney General, Eric Holder, even referred to himself as "Obama's wingman."

LXXVI. THE APPOINTING POWER OF THE EXECUTIVE

The institution of delegated power implies, that there is a portion of virtue and honor among mankind, which may be a reasonable foundation of confidence; and experience justifies the theory. It has been found to exist in the most corrupt periods of the most corrupt governments.

76. Public Virtue

Cynics have observed that the careful dispersal of power and the system of checks and balances in our government presuppose a tendency to evil. It is supposed that elected officials will naturally try to accumulate more power than they should. There is certainly an element of truth in this observation. This excerpt, however, points to the opposite principle, namely, that the public places .and is justified in placing great trust in the hands of its elected representatives. A further corollary is that there is a repository of virtue and goodness in the citizenry that makes them capable of electing good and virtuous leaders at least most of the time.

LXXVIII. THE JUDICIARY DEPARTMENT

(T)he judiciary, from the nature of its functions, will always be the least dangerous to the political rights of the Constitution: because it will be least in a capacity to annoy or injure them . . .

(T)hough individual oppression may now and then proceed from the courts of justice, the general liberty of the people can never be endangered from that quarter; I mean so long as the judiciary remains truly distinct from both the legislative and the Executive. For I agree, that "there is no liberty if the power of judging be not separated from the legislative and executive powers."

78. Judicial Activism

The author could not anticipate the breadth of modern judicial activism. The key here is clear separation of powers. Modern judicial activism has been taken to such an extreme that courts have even ordered new property taxes in order to accomplish court-ordered changes in school systems, truly taxation without representation and legislation without accountability. Except when voiding legislation due to unconstitutionality and according to criteria of strict adherence to the Constitution, to substitute an individual judge's view for the will of the elected legislature—even if its imperfect writing results in less than perfect or unintended results—is to impose judicial tyranny of the worst sort and to destroy the rule of law.

LXXVIII. THE JUDICIARY DEPARTMENT

The complete independence of the courts of justice is peculiarly essential in a limited Constitution. By a limited Constitution, I understand one which contains certain specified exceptions to the legislative authority; such, for instance, as that it shall pass no bills of attainder, no *ex-post-facto* laws, and the like. Limitations of this kind can be preserved in practice no other way than through the medium of courts of justice, whose duty it must be to declare all acts contrary to the manifest tenor of the Constitution void. . . .

To avoid an arbitrary discretion in the courts, it is indispensable that they should be bound down by strict rules and precedents, which serve to define and point out their duty in every particular case that comes before them; and it will readily be conceived from the variety of controversies which grow out of the folly and wickedness of mankind, that the records of those precedents must unavoidably swell to a very considerable bulk and must demand long and laborious study to acquire a competent knowledge of them. Hence it is, that there can be but few men in the society who will have sufficient skill in the laws to qualify them for the stations of judges.

78. Limited Government

The ability of the courts to void laws is a vital check on the other branches of government and a support for the rule of law, but it is effective only if the Constitution is strictly interpreted and adhered to. That is the clear meaning of not going contrary to the "manifest tenor" of it. Those who would wrest the meaning of that document should recall that the Declaration of Independence also was accepted as the Supreme Law of the Land. That great document includes the following lines: "We hold these truths to be self-evident, that all men are created equal, that they are endowed by their creator with certain unalienable rights, that among these are life, liberty, and the pursuit of happiness—That to secure these rights, governments are instituted among men, deriving their just powers from the consent of the governed, *that whenever any form of government becomes destructive of these ends, it is the right of the people to alter or to abolish it, and to institute a new government*, laying its foundation on such principles, and organizing its powers in such form, as to them shall seem most likely to effect their safety and happiness" (italics added).

LXXI. THE JUDICIARY CONTINUED, AND THE DISTRIBUTION OF THE JUDICIAL AUTHORITY

Particular misconstructions and contraventions of the will of the legislature may now and then happen; but they can never be so extensive as to amount to an inconvenience, or in any sensible degree to affect the order of the political system. This may be inferred with certainty, from the general nature of the judicial power, from the objects to which it relates, from the manner in which it is exercised, from its comparative weakness, and from its total incapacity to support its usurpations by force.

81. Judicial Activism

Here again Hamilton was being overly optimistic, or rather he underestimated the imagination of judges. Preventing judicial excess has become a major concern for legislature and executive. But in defense of the courts, "contraventions" of the will of the legislature often result not because the courts misinterpret or are opposed to the legislation as originally written, but rather because the much more extensive rules, regulations, and procedures based on that legislation go beyond it and themselves misconstrue the intent. In some cases this may even by the hidden agenda of some legislators, to avoid dealing with difficult issues by deferring to bureaucrats to secretly work out the details and to judges to settle their legality. Bizarre extrapolations of environmental legislation resulting in uncompensated loss of property rights may fall into this category.

LXXXII. THE JUDICIARY CONTINUED, AND THE DISTRIBUTION OF THE JUDICIAL AUTHORITY

The principles established in a former paper teach us that the States will retain all *preexisting* authorities which may not be exclusively delegated to the federal head; and that this exclusive delegation can only exist in one of three cases: where an exclusive authority is, in express terms, granted to the Union; or where a particular authority is granted to the Union, and the exercise of a like authority is prohibited to the States; or where an authority is granted to the Union, with which a similar authority in the States would be utterly incompatible.

82. States' Rights

Here again, only limited authority is delegated to the federal government. Powers which it exercises beyond these are without authority.

LXXXIII. THE JUDICIARY CONTINUED IN RELATION TO TRIAL BY JURY

The rules of legal interpretation are rules of *common-sense*, adopted by the courts in the construction of the laws.

83. Justice

It is apparent to the ordinary citizen that common sense has been disregarded in favor of ideology and theory in much of modern America's legal system, particularly as pertains to civil rights in criminal justice settings, mandatory sentencing, and in the handling of violent crime and juveniles.

LXXXIII. THE JUDICIARY CONTINUED IN RELATION TO TRIAL BY JURY

The plan of the convention declares that the power of Congress, or, in other words, of the *national legislature*, shall extend to certain enumerated cases. This specification of particulars evidently excludes all pretensions to a general legislative authority, because an affirmative grant of special powers would be absurd, as well as useless, if a general authority was intended.

83. Limited Government

The authors of the Constitution reassure us that the federal government will have only limited powers. Those powers must be specified precisely because no "general legislative authority" is given. And yet, Congress in our day is so arrogant as to suppose that it or its bureaucratic substitutes can legislate the minutiae of business transactions, manufacturing, visits to the doctor, and even the quantity of water per flush of a toilet.

LXXXIII. THE JUDICIARY CONTINUED IN RELATION TO TRIAL BY JURY

It has been observed, that trial by jury is a

safeguard against an oppressive exercise of the power of taxation. This observation deserves to be canvassed. It is evident that it can have no influence upon the legislature, in regard to the *amount* of taxes to be laid, to the *objects* upon which they are to be imposed, or to the *rule* by which they are to be apportioned. If it can have any influence, therefore, it must be upon the mode of collection, and the conduct of the officers intrusted with the execution of the revenue laws.

83. Independent Agencies

It was expected that offenses by tax collectors would be tried by jury. Tax collectors, which today would include auditors, were to be held accountable for their actions and if guilty of extortion, harassment, or other inappropriate behaviors could be punished in criminal court. The usual modern immunity of the IRS to legal recourse by its victims is contrary to the intent of the founders. This quotation also touches on another matter, more particularly important when the taxpayer is the defendant, namely the great power of juries to void laws by refusing to find offenders of them guilty—nullification.

LXXXIII. THE JUDICIARY CONTINUED IN RELATION TO TRIAL BY JURY

The nature of a court of equity will readily

permit the extension of its jurisdiction to matters of law; but it is not a little to be suspected, that the attempt to extend the jurisdiction of the courts of law to matters of equity will not be unproductive of the advantages which may be derived from courts of chancery, on the plan upon which they are established in this State, but will tend gradually to change the nature of the courts of law, and to undermine the trial by jury, by introducing questions too complicated for a decision in that mode.

83. Justice

It is not necessary for our purposes to distinguish between courts of equity and chancery, but to make note of the last few phrases in this quotation. Namely, there is a danger of undermining the value of jury trials by introducing to them excessively complicated legal questions, ones which are properly decided by judges (see Paper # LXXVIII above). The introduction of complicated legal issues as a defense for individuals whose guilt is plainly manifest is one of the problems that have reduced the integrity and value of the judicial system in the minds of many citizens.

LXXXIV. CERTAIN GENERAL AND MISCELLANEOUS OBJECTIONS TO THE CONSTITUTION CONSIDERED AND ANSWERED

The establishment of the writ of *habeas corpus*, the prohibition of *ex-post-facto* laws, and of TITLES OF NOBILITY, *to which we have no corresponding provisions in our* (state) *Constitution*, are perhaps greater securities to liberty and republicanism than any it contains. The creation of crimes after the commission of the fact, or, in other words, the subjecting of men to punishment for things which, when they were done, were breaches of no law, and the practice of arbitrary imprisonments, have been, in all ages, the favorite and most formidable instruments of tyranny.

84. Justice

The principle of having a writ is tied to the concept that the execution of justice should be swift, sure, and fair. A writ requires probable cause, thus increasing the likelihood that one arrested will in fact be prosecuted, convicted, and punished. And yet, our modern justice system has become so mired in triviality, disproportionality, and the unjust maneuverings of lawyers that the time between crime and arrest and trial has become inordinately prolonged. Consider the California case of a man accused of abusing children in a day-care center. The charges proved spurious and the man was acquitted, but only after two years of being held in jail without bail. In the meantime, others, even repeat offenders of undisputed guilt, were rapidly paroled because of court-defined jail over-crowding. Even murderers, including those guilty of the most heinous crimes, languish many years on death row while streams of lawyers pursue serial appeals on technical issues at taxpayer expense and to the detriment of the legal system.

LXXIV. CERTAIN GENERAL AND MISCELLANEOUS OBJECTIONS TO THE CONSTITUTION CONSIDERED AND ANSWERED

Nothing need be said to illustrate the importance of the prohibition of titles of nobility. This may truly be denominated the cornerstone of republican government; for so long as they are excluded, there can never be serious danger that the government will be any other than that of the people.

84. Arrogance of Government

The prohibition of titles of nobility was more

acutely recognized as an important principle by the founding fathers, who had grown up in the shadow of the stratified European system with its aristocratic few and subservient many. It was desired by them that freedom of opportunity would create a "natural aristocracy" based on the inherent ability and diligence of the individual. Frequent elections and ample opportunities for public service would enable such people to develop and use their talents in the political arena just as freedom of association, of speech, and so forth would enable them to develop and perform in the private sector.

But in our day legislators typically remain in office for decades; are exempt from the great bulk of laws and regulations placed on their fellow citizens; are granted enormous perks, privileges, and pensions which otherwise would not be available to any but the wealthiest; and are even permitted to accumulate large sums of money partially at taxpayer expense to be used for their campaigns, thus maintaining their hold on office. What are these people but an oligarchy, who, when their power and position are passed on in the family (not a rare occurrence) become an aristocracy? And what are the words *senator* and *congressman* if not titles of nobility when accompanied by all the arrogance and pride of *duke* or *earl*?

LXXXIV. CERTAIN GENERAL AND MISCELLANEOUS OBJECTIONS TO THE CONSTITUTION CONSIDERED AND ANSWERED

It has been several times truly remarked that bills of rights are, in their origin, stipulations between kings and their subjects, abridgements of prerogative in favor of privilege, reservations of rights not surrendered to the prince . . . Here, in strictness, the people surrender nothing; and as they retain everything they have no need of particular reservations. "WE, THE PEOPLE of the United States, to secure the blessings of liberty to ourselves and our posterity, do *ordain* and *establish* this Constitution for the United States of America." Here is a better recognition of popular rights, than volumes of those aphorisms which make the principal figure in several of our State bills of rights, and which would sound much better in a treatise of ethics than in a constitution of government.

But a minute detail of particular rights is certainly far less applicable to a Constitution like that under consideration, which is merely intended to regulate the general political interests of the nation, than to a constitution which has the regulation of every species of personal and private concerns . . .

I go further, and affirm that bills of rights, in the sense and to the extent in which they are contended for, are not only unnecessary in the proposed Constitution, but would even be dangerous. They would contain various exceptions to powers not granted; and, on this very account, would afford a colorable pretext to claim more than were granted. For why declare that things shall not be done which there is no power to do?

84. Limited Government

A Bill of Rights was attached to the Constitution in order to reassure the anti-federalists and others who were afraid of the power of the new government. Hamilton was philosophically correct, of course, and the fear he expressed in the last paragraph above has been thoroughly justified, but thank heavens he lost on this point. Even those specific items which were included in the Bill of Rights are under assault, and there is widespread belief in the ultimate power of government, power which was never granted by the people, where it rightly resides.

LXXXIV. CERTAIN GENERAL AND MISCELLANEOUS OBJECTIONS TO THE CONSTITUTION CONSIDERED AND ANSWERED

Whence is the dreaded augmentation of expense to spring? One source indicated, is the multiplication of offices under the new government . .

But upon no reasonable plan can it amount to a sum which would be an object of material consequence . . .

Hence it is evident that a portion of the year will suffice for the session of both the Senate and the House of Representatives; we may suppose about one-fourth for the latter and one-third or perhaps one-half, for the former . . .

The result from these observations is that the sources of additional expense from the establishment of the proposed Constitution are much fewer than may have been imagined.

84. Limited Government

The "augmentation of offices" has gone far beyond what Hamilton could have imagined. In 1994 America reached a milestone of sorts when the number of non-military government employees exceeded the number of manufacturing workers, and it has grown much worse since then. To pay for these legions and the programs they administer, the taxpayers sent Washington in fiscal 2015 a record 3.3 trillion dollars ($3,300,000,000,000.00) and they still ran a budget deficit measured in the hundreds of billions. The accumulated national debt in 2015 was over 19 trillion dollars, with unfunded liabilities bringing the total to over 123 trillion. Such astronomical figures indicate unlimited government run amuck; they are debts hung around the necks of our unborn descendents. *Milestone*? Perhaps *millstone* would be more accurate.

LXXXV. CONCLUDING REMARKS

(There is an) utter improbability of assembling a new convention, under circumstances in any degree so favorable to a happy issue, as those in which the late convention met, deliberated, and concluded . . .

The establishment of a Constitution, in time of profound peace, by the voluntary consent of a whole people, is a prodigy, to the completion of which I look forward with trembling anxiety.

85. Renewing The Heritage of the Founding Fathers

That this was true in the months following the Constitutional Convention, when most of the founders were still alive, is further caution to the danger of attempting a new convention now. Who are the Madison, Hamilton, and Adams of our day? Where is the General Washington who will preside gravely over the meeting? It is tempting to think that all the errors of the past century could be solved at one grand convention in which two or three or four specific amendments were debated and passed, but there is danger that such a gathering could deteriorate and leave us no better at best or fallen into anarchy at worst. Nevertheless, under Article V, if Congress is unable to pass appropriate amendments, a supermajority of states may call a convention for that purpose.

Amendments are one thing, a more thorough-going renewal is another, deeper, longer-term process. It goes to the question of what it is that makes an American, American—not location, ethnicity, race, or origin, but rather adherence to principles of personal freedom, individual ingenuity, and self-reliance. Nowhere are those ideals more concisely and clearly expressed than in the Constitution, the Bill of Rights, and the Declaration of Independence.

Renewal requires education of young and old, re-examination of the founding documents and the arguments for and against them, and a thoughtful rejection of so-called "progressive" doctrines which at their heart are anti-American, meaning opposed to the principles that made Americans uniquely distinguishable from others around the world. *Progressive* has been revived as a label, borrowed from the turn of the 19th century to replace the discredited term *liberal*; it is an unexamined term that assumes "progress" is an ideal, without consideration of what one progresses toward; it is a godless millennial term that supposes mankind can create a perfect society of perfect people in a modern Eden, but in practice is always an excuse for an elite few to rule without restraint over the non-elite many.

On the political level, renewal can be effected by the states reasserting their individual and collective authority not only over themselves, but over the Union itself in those matters not delegated to it. This can be accomplished only by careful selection at state and local levels of candidates who understand and are committed to the principles of individual liberty and federalism, as well as by promotion of like-minded people on the national level.

John O'Sullivan cited Macaulay's description of England on the eve of their revolution, "(Is) anything more terrible than the situation of a government which rules . . . over a people of hypocrites, which is flattered by the press and cursed in the inner chambers?" Alas, that such conditions prevail in 21st century America! Thanks to the good work of the founding fathers, we have the means to move beyond such conditions by applying the principles they taught us, tempered by the lessons of "Schoolmaster History".

Ultimate political power in this nation remains with the people, who not only elect to office, but with election also remove from office. To wield such power the people must be reminded of its proper use in the context of the inspired American Constitution, for it is this power that must be invoked for a peaceful renewal of constitutional government.

THE CONSTITUTION

OF THE UNITED STATES OF AMERICA

(Underlined sentences have been deleted or altered by subsequent amendment.)

We the People of the United States, in Order to form a more perfect Union, establish Justice, insure domestic Tranquility, provide for the common defence, promote the general Welfare, and secure the Blessings of Liberty to ourselves and our Posterity, do ordain and establish this Constitution for the United States of America.

Article. I.

Section. 1.

All legislative Powers herein granted shall be vested in a Congress of the United States, which shall consist of a Senate and House of Representatives.

Section. 2.

The House of Representatives shall be composed of Members chosen every second Year by the People of the several States, and the Electors in each State shall have the Qualifications requisite for Electors of the most numerous Branch of the State Legislature.

No Person shall be a Representative who shall not have attained to the Age of twenty five Years, and been seven Years a Citizen of the United States, and who shall not, when elected, be an Inhabitant of that State in which he shall be chosen.

Representatives and direct Taxes shall be apportioned among the several States which may be included within this Union, according to their respective Numbers, which shall be determined by adding to the whole Number of free Persons, including those bound to Service for a Term of Years, and excluding Indians not taxed, three fifths of all other Persons. The actual Enumeration shall be made within three Years after the first Meeting of the Congress of the United States, and within every subsequent Term of ten Years, in such Manner as they shall by Law direct. The Number of Representatives shall not exceed one for every thirty Thousand, but each State shall have at Least one Representative; and until such enumeration shall be made, the State of New Hampshire shall be entitled to chuse three, Massachusetts eight, Rhode-Island and Providence Plantations one, Connecticut five, New-York six, New Jersey four, Pennsylvania eight,

Delaware one, Maryland six, Virginia ten, North Carolina five, South Carolina five, and Georgia three.

When vacancies happen in the Representation from any State, the Executive Authority thereof shall issue Writs of Election to fill such Vacancies.

The House of Representatives shall chuse their Speaker and other Officers; and shall have the sole Power of Impeachment.

Section. 3.

The Senate of the United States shall be composed of two Senators from each State, <u>chosen by the Legislature</u> thereof, for six Years; and each Senator shall have one Vote.

Immediately after they shall be assembled in Consequence of the first Election, they shall be divided as equally as may be into three Classes. The Seats of the Senators of the first Class shall be vacated at the Expiration of the second Year, of the second Class at the Expiration of the fourth Year, and of the third Class at the Expiration of the sixth Year, so that one third may be chosen every second Year; <u>and if Vacancies happen by Resignation, or otherwise, during the Recess of the Legislature of any State, the Executive thereof may make temporary Appointments until the next Meeting of the Legislature, which shall then fill such Vacancies.</u>

No Person shall be a Senator who shall not have attained to the Age of thirty Years, and been nine Years a Citizen of the United States, and who shall not, when elected, be an Inhabitant of that State for which he shall be chosen.

The Vice President of the United States shall be President of the Senate, but shall have no Vote, unless they be equally divided.

The Senate shall chuse their other Officers, and also a President pro tempore, in the Absence of the Vice President, or when he shall exercise the Office of President of the United States.

The Senate shall have the sole Power to try all Impeachments. When sitting for that Purpose, they shall be on Oath or Affirmation. When the President of the United States is tried, the Chief Justice shall preside: And no Person shall be convicted without the Concurrence of two thirds of the Members present.

Judgment in Cases of Impeachment shall not extend further than to removal from Office, and disqualification to hold and enjoy any Office of honor, Trust or Profit under the United States: but the Party convicted shall nevertheless be liable and subject to Indictment, Trial, Judgment and Punishment, according to Law.

Section. 4.

The Times, Places and Manner of holding Elections for Senators and Representatives, shall be prescribed in each State by the Legislature thereof; but the Congress may at any time by Law make or alter such Regulations, except as to the Places of chusing Senators.

The Congress shall assemble at least once in every Year, and such Meeting shall <u>be on the first Monday in December</u>, unless they shall by Law appoint a different Day.

Section. 5.

Each House shall be the Judge of the Elections, Returns and Qualifications of its own Members, and a Majority of each shall constitute a Quorum to do Business; but a smaller Number may adjourn from day to day, and may be authorized to compel the Attendance of absent Members, in such Manner, and under such Penalties as each House may provide.

Each House may determine the Rules of its Proceedings, punish its Members for disorderly Behaviour, and, with the Concurrence of two thirds, expel a Member.

Each House shall keep a Journal of its Proceedings, and from time to time publish the same, excepting such Parts as may in their Judgment require Secrecy; and the Yeas and Nays of the Members of either House on any question shall, at the Desire of one fifth of those Present, be entered on the Journal.

Neither House, during the Session of Congress, shall, without the Consent of the other, adjourn for more than three days, nor to any other Place than that in which the two Houses shall be sitting.

Section. 6.

The Senators and Representatives shall receive a Compensation for their Services, to be ascertained by

Law, and paid out of the Treasury of the United States. They shall in all Cases, except Treason, Felony and Breach of the Peace, be privileged from Arrest during their Attendance at the Session of their respective Houses, and in going to and returning from the same; and for any Speech or Debate in either House, they shall not be questioned in any other Place.

No Senator or Representative shall, during the Time for which he was elected, be appointed to any civil Office under the Authority of the United States, which shall have been created, or the Emoluments whereof shall have been encreased during such time; and no Person holding any Office under the United States, shall be a Member of either House during his Continuance in Office.

Section. 7.

All Bills for raising Revenue shall originate in the House of Representatives; but the Senate may propose or concur with Amendments as on other Bills.

Every Bill which shall have passed the House of Representatives and the Senate, shall, before it become a Law, be presented to the President of the United States; If he approve he shall sign it, but if not he shall return it, with his Objections to that House in which it shall have originated, who shall enter the Objections at large on their Journal, and proceed to reconsider it. If after such Reconsideration two thirds of that House shall agree to pass the Bill, it shall be sent, together with the Objections, to the other House, by which it shall likewise be reconsidered, and if approved by two thirds of that House, it shall become a Law. But in all such Cases the Votes of both Houses shall be determined by yeas and Nays, and the Names of the Persons voting for and against the Bill shall be entered on the Journal of each House respectively. If any Bill shall not be returned by the President within ten Days (Sundays excepted) after it shall have been presented to him, the Same shall be a Law, in like Manner as if he had signed it, unless the Congress by their Adjournment prevent its Return, in which Case it shall not be a Law.

Every Order, Resolution, or Vote to which the Concurrence of the Senate and House of Representatives may be necessary (except on a question of Adjournment) shall be presented to the President of the United States; and before the Same shall take Effect, shall be approved by him, or being disapproved by him, shall be repassed by two thirds of the Senate and House of Representatives, according to the Rules and Limitations prescribed in the Case of a Bill.

Section. 8.

The Congress shall have Power To lay and collect Taxes, Duties, Imposts and Excises, to pay the Debts and provide for the common Defence and general Welfare of the United States; but all Duties, Imposts and Excises shall be uniform throughout the United States;

To borrow Money on the credit of the United States;

To regulate Commerce with foreign Nations, and among the several States, and with the Indian Tribes;

To establish an uniform Rule of Naturalization, and uniform Laws on the subject of Bankruptcies throughout the United States;

To coin Money, regulate the Value thereof, and of foreign Coin, and fix the Standard of Weights and Measures;

To provide for the Punishment of counterfeiting the Securities and current Coin of the United States;

To establish Post Offices and post Roads;

To promote the Progress of Science and useful Arts, by securing for limited Times to Authors and Inventors the exclusive Right to their respective Writings and Discoveries;

To constitute Tribunals inferior to the supreme Court;

To define and punish Piracies and Felonies committed on the high Seas, and Offences against the Law of Nations;

To declare War, grant Letters of Marque and Reprisal, and make Rules concerning Captures on Land and Water;

To raise and support Armies, but no Appropriation of Money to that Use shall be for a longer Term than two Years;

To provide and maintain a Navy;

To make Rules for the Government and Regulation of the land and naval Forces;

To provide for calling forth the Militia to execute the Laws of the Union, suppress Insurrections and repel Invasions;

To provide for organizing, arming, and disciplining, the Militia, and for governing such Part of them as may be employed in the Service of the United States, reserving to the States respectively, the Appointment of the Officers, and the Authority of training the Militia according to the discipline prescribed by Congress;

To exercise exclusive Legislation in all Cases whatsoever, over such District (not exceeding ten Miles square) as may, by Cession of particular States, and the Acceptance of Congress, become the Seat of the Government of the United States, and to exercise like Authority over all Places purchased by the Consent of the Legislature of the State in which the Same shall be, for the Erection of Forts, Magazines, Arsenals, dock-Yards, and other needful Buildings;—And

To make all Laws which shall be necessary and proper for carrying into Execution the foregoing Powers, and all other Powers vested by this Constitution in the Government of the United States, or in any Department or Officer thereof.

Section. 9.

The Migration or Importation of such Persons as any of the States now existing shall think proper to admit, shall not be prohibited by the Congress prior to the Year one thousand eight hundred and eight, but a Tax or duty may be imposed on such Importation, not exceeding ten dollars for each Person.

The Privilege of the Writ of Habeas Corpus shall not be suspended, unless when in Cases of Rebellion or Invasion the public Safety may require it.

No Bill of Attainder or ex post facto Law shall be passed.

No Capitation, or other direct, Tax shall be laid, <u>unless in Proportion to the Census or enumeration herein before directed to be taken.</u>

No Tax or Duty shall be laid on Articles exported from any State.

No Preference shall be given by any Regulation of Commerce or Revenue to the Ports of one State over those of another: nor shall Vessels bound to, or from, one State, be obliged to enter, clear, or pay Duties in another.

No Money shall be drawn from the Treasury, but in Consequence of Appropriations made by Law; and a regular Statement and Account of the Receipts and Expenditures of all public Money shall be published from time to time.

No Title of Nobility shall be granted by the United States: And no Person holding any Office of Profit or Trust under them, shall, without the Consent of the Congress, accept of any present, Emolument, Office, or Title, of any kind whatever, from any King, Prince, or foreign State.

Section. 10.

No State shall enter into any Treaty, Alliance, or Confederation; grant Letters of Marque and Reprisal; coin Money; emit Bills of Credit; make any Thing but gold and silver Coin a Tender in Payment of Debts; pass any Bill of Attainder, ex post facto Law, or Law impairing the Obligation of Contracts, or grant any Title of Nobility.

No State shall, without the Consent of the Congress, lay any Imposts or Duties on Imports or Exports, except what may be absolutely necessary for executing it's inspection Laws: and the net Produce of all Duties and Imposts, laid by any State on Imports or Exports, shall be for the Use of the Treasury of the United States; and all such Laws shall be subject to the Revision and Controul of the Congress.

No State shall, without the Consent of Congress, lay any Duty of Tonnage, keep Troops, or Ships of War in time of Peace, enter into any Agreement or Compact with another State, or with a foreign Power, or engage in War, unless actually invaded, or in such imminent Danger as will not admit of delay.

Article. II.

Section. 1.

The executive Power shall be vested in a President of the United States of America. He shall hold his Office during the Term of four Years, and, together with the Vice President, chosen for the same Term, be elected, as follows

Each State shall appoint, in such Manner as the Legislature thereof may direct, a Number of Electors, equal to the whole Number of Senators and Representatives to which the State may be entitled in the Congress: but no Senator or Representative, or Person holding an Office of Trust or Profit under the United States, shall be appointed an Elector.

The Electors shall meet in their respective States, and vote by Ballot for two Persons, of whom one at least shall not be an Inhabitant of the same State with themselves. And they shall make a List of all the Persons voted for, and of the Number of Votes for each; which List they shall sign and certify, and transmit sealed to the Seat of the Government of the United States, directed to the President of the Senate. The President of the Senate shall, in the Presence of the Senate and House of Representatives, open all the Certificates, and the Votes shall then be counted. The Person having the greatest Number of Votes shall be the President, if such Number be a Majority of the whole Number of Electors appointed; and if there be more than one who have such Majority, and have an equal Number of Votes, then the House of Representatives shall immediately chuse by Ballot one of them for President; and if no Person have a Majority, then from the five highest on the List the said House shall in like Manner chuse the President. But in chusing the President, the Votes shall be taken by States, the Representation from each State having one Vote; A quorum for this Purpose shall consist of a Member or Members from two thirds of the States, and a Majority of all the States shall be necessary to a Choice. In every Case, after the Choice of the President, the Person having the greatest Number of Votes of the Electors shall be the Vice President. But if there should remain two or more who have equal Votes, the Senate shall chuse from them by Ballot the Vice President.

The Congress may determine the Time of chusing the Electors, and the Day on which they shall give their Votes; which Day shall be the same throughout the United States.

No Person except a natural born Citizen, or a Citizen of the United States, at the time of the Adoption of this Constitution, shall be eligible to the Office of President; neither shall any Person be eligible to that Office who shall not have attained to the Age of thirty five Years, and been fourteen Years a Resident within the United States.

In Case of the Removal of the President from Office, or of his Death, Resignation, or Inability to discharge the Powers and Duties of the said Office, the Same shall devolve on the Vice President, and the Congress may by Law provide for the Case of Removal, Death, Resignation or Inability, both of the President and Vice President, declaring what Officer shall then act as President, and such Officer shall act accordingly, until the Disability be removed, or a President shall be elected.

The President shall, at stated Times, receive for his Services, a Compensation, which shall neither be encreased nor diminished during the Period for which he shall have been elected, and he shall not receive within that Period any other Emolument from the United States, or any of them.

Before he enter on the Execution of his Office, he shall take the following Oath or Affirmation:—"I do solemnly swear (or affirm) that I will faithfully execute the Office of President of the United States, and will to the best of my Ability, preserve, protect and defend the Constitution of the United States."

Section. 2.

The President shall be Commander in Chief of the Army and Navy of the United States, and of the Militia of the several States, when called into the actual Service of the United States; he may require the Opinion, in writing, of the principal Officer in each of the executive Departments, upon any Subject relating to the Duties of their respective Offices, and he shall have Power to grant Reprieves and Pardons for Offences against the United States, except in Cases of Impeachment.

He shall have Power, by and with the Advice and Consent of the Senate, to make Treaties, provided two thirds of the Senators present concur; and he shall nominate, and by and with the Advice and Consent of the Senate, shall appoint Ambassadors, other public Ministers and Consuls, Judges of the supreme Court, and all other Officers of the United States, whose Appointments are not herein otherwise provided for, and which shall be established by Law: but the Congress may by Law vest the Appointment of such inferior Officers, as they think proper, in the President alone, in the Courts of Law, or in the Heads of Departments.

The President shall have Power to fill up all Vacancies that may happen during the Recess of the Senate, by granting Commissions which shall expire at the End of their next Session.

Section. 3.

He shall from time to time give to the Congress Information of the State of the Union, and recommend to their Consideration such Measures as he shall judge necessary and expedient; he may, on extraordinary Occasions, convene both Houses, or either of them, and in Case of Disagreement between them, with Respect to the Time of Adjournment, he may adjourn them to such Time as he shall think proper; he shall receive Ambassadors and other public Ministers; he shall take Care that the Laws be faithfully executed, and shall Commission all the Officers of the United States.

Section. 4.

The President, Vice President and all civil Officers of the United States, shall be removed from Office on Impeachment for, and Conviction of, Treason, Bribery, or other high Crimes and Misdemeanors.

Article III.

Section. 1.

The judicial Power of the United States, shall be vested in one supreme Court, and in such inferior Courts as the Congress may from time to time ordain and establish. The Judges, both of the supreme and inferior Courts, shall hold their Offices during good Behaviour, and shall, at stated Times, receive for their Services, a Compensation, which shall not be diminished during their Continuance in Office.

Section. 2.

The judicial Power shall extend to all Cases, in Law and Equity, arising under this Constitution, the Laws of the United States, and Treaties made, or which shall be made, under their Authority;—to all Cases affecting Ambassadors, other public Ministers and Consuls;—to all Cases of admiralty and maritime Jurisdiction;—to Controversies to which the United States shall be a Party;—to Controversies between two or more States;— between a State and Citizens of another State,— between Citizens of different States,—between Citizens of the same State claiming Lands under Grants of different States, and between a State, or the Citizens thereof, and foreign States, Citizens or Subjects.

In all Cases affecting Ambassadors, other public Ministers and Consuls, and those in which a State shall be Party, the supreme Court shall have original Jurisdiction. In all the other Cases before mentioned, the supreme Court shall have appellate Jurisdiction, both as to Law and Fact, with such Exceptions, and under such Regulations as the Congress shall make.

The Trial of all Crimes, except in Cases of Impeachment, shall be by Jury; and such Trial shall be held in the State where the said Crimes shall have been committed; but when not committed within any State, the Trial shall be at such Place or Places as the Congress may by Law have directed.

Section. 3.

Treason against the United States, shall consist only in levying War against them, or in adhering to their Enemies, giving them Aid and Comfort. No Person shall be convicted of Treason unless on the Testimony of two Witnesses to the same overt Act, or on Confession in open Court.

The Congress shall have Power to declare the Punishment of Treason, but no Attainder of Treason shall work Corruption of Blood, or Forfeiture except during the Life of the Person attainted.

Article. IV.

Section. 1.

Full Faith and Credit shall be given in each State to the public Acts, Records, and judicial Proceedings of every other State. And the Congress may by general Laws prescribe the Manner in which such Acts, Records and Proceedings shall be proved, and the Effect thereof.

Section. 2.

The Citizens of each State shall be entitled to all Privileges and Immunities of Citizens in the several States.

A Person charged in any State with Treason, Felony, or other Crime, who shall flee from Justice, and be found in another State, shall on Demand of the executive Authority of the State from which he fled, be delivered up, to be removed to the State having Jurisdiction of the Crime.

No Person held to Service or Labour in one State, under the Laws thereof, escaping into another, shall, in Consequence of any Law or Regulation therein, be discharged from such Service or Labour, but shall be delivered up on Claim of the Party to whom such Service or Labour may be due.

Section. 3.

New States may be admitted by the Congress into this Union; but no new State shall be formed or erected within the Jurisdiction of any other State; nor any State be formed by the Junction of two or more States, or Parts of States, without the Consent of the Legislatures of the States concerned as well as of the Congress.

The Congress shall have Power to dispose of and make all needful Rules and Regulations respecting the Territory or other Property belonging to the United States; and nothing in this Constitution shall be so construed as to Prejudice any Claims of the United States, or of any particular State.

Section. 4.

The United States shall guarantee to every State in this Union a Republican Form of Government, and shall protect each of them against Invasion; and on Application of the Legislature, or of the Executive (when the Legislature cannot be convened), against domestic Violence.

Article. V.

The Congress, whenever two thirds of both Houses shall deem it necessary, shall propose Amendments to this Constitution, or, on the Application of the Legislatures of two thirds of the several States, shall call a Convention for proposing Amendments, which, in either Case, shall be valid to all Intents and Purposes, as Part of this Constitution, when ratified by the Legislatures of three fourths of the several States, or by Conventions in three fourths thereof, as the one or the other Mode of Ratification may be proposed by the Congress; Provided that no Amendment which may be made prior to the Year One thousand eight hundred and eight shall in any Manner affect the first and fourth Clauses in the Ninth Section of the first Article; and that no State, without its Consent, shall be deprived of its equal Suffrage in the Senate.

Article. VI.

All Debts contracted and Engagements entered into, before the Adoption of this Constitution, shall be as valid against the United States under this Constitution, as under the Confederation.

This Constitution, and the Laws of the United States which shall be made in Pursuance thereof; and all Treaties made, or which shall be made, under the

Authority of the United States, shall be the supreme Law of the Land; and the Judges in every State shall be bound thereby, any Thing in the Constitution or Laws of any State to the Contrary notwithstanding.

The Senators and Representatives before mentioned, and the Members of the several State Legislatures, and all executive and judicial Officers, both of the United States and of the several States, shall be bound by Oath or Affirmation, to support this Constitution; but no religious Test shall ever be required as a Qualification to any Office or public Trust under the United States.

Article. VII.

The Ratification of the Conventions of nine States, shall be sufficient for the Establishment of this Constitution between the States so ratifying the Same.

The Word, "the," being interlined between the seventh and eighth Lines of the first Page, The Word "Thirty" being partly written on an Erazure in the fifteenth Line of the first Page, The Words "is tried" being interlined between the thirty second and thirty third Lines of the first Page and the Word "the" being interlined between the forty third and forty fourth Lines of the second Page.

Attest William Jackson Secretary

done in Convention by the Unanimous Consent of the States present the Seventeenth Day of September in the Year of our Lord one thousand seven hundred and Eighty seven and of the Independance of the United States of America the Twelfth In witness whereof We have hereunto subscribed our Names,

G°. Washington
Presidt and deputy from Virginia

Delaware
Geo: Read
Gunning Bedford jun
John Dickinson
Richard Bassett
Jaco: Broom

Maryland
James McHenry
Dan of St Thos.
Jenifer
Danl. Carroll

Virginia
John Blair
James Madison Jr.

North Carolina
Wm. Blount
Richd. Dobbs Spaight
Hu Williamson

South Carolina
J. Rutledge
Charles Cotesworth
Pinckney
Charles Pinckney
Pierce Butler

Georgia
William Few
Abr Baldwin

New Hampshire
John Langdon
Nicholas Gilman

Massachusetts
Nathaniel Gorham
Rufus King

Connecticut
Wm. Saml. Johnson
Roger Sherman

New York
Alexander Hamilton

New Jersey
Wil: Livingston
David Brearley
Wm. Paterson
Jona: Dayton

Pensylvania
B Franklin
Thomas Mifflin
Robt. Morris
Geo. Clymer
Thos. FitzSimons
Jared Ingersoll
James Wilson
Gouv Morris

There are many excellent websites that feature the Constitution and provide information about its history and meaning. This is a particularly good one:

http://www.archives.gov/exhibits/charters/print_friendly.html?page=co
nstitution_transcript_content.html&title=The%20Constitution%20of%
20the%20United%20States%3A%20A%20Transcription

Bill of Rights

and Other Amendments to The Constitution

The Ten Original Amendments: The Bill of Rights. Passed by Congress September 25, 1789. Ratified December 15, 1791.

1. Congress shall make no law respecting an establishment of religion, or prohibiting the free exercise thereof; or abridging the freedom of speech, or of the press; or the right of the people peaceably to assemble, and to petition the government for a redress of grievances.
2. A well regulated Militia, being necessary to the security of a free State, the right of the people to keep and bear Arms, shall not be infringed.
3. No Soldier shall, in time of peace be quartered in any house, without the consent of the Owner, nor in time of war, but in a manner to be prescribed by law.
4. The right of the people to be secure in their persons, houses, papers, and effects, against unreasonable searches and seizures, shall not be violated, and no Warrants shall issue, but upon probable cause, supported by Oath or affirmation, and particularly describing the place to be searched, and the persons or things to be seized.
5. No person shall be held to answer for a capital, or otherwise infamous crime, unless on a presentment or indictment of a Grand Jury, except in cases arising in the land or naval forces, or in the Militia, when in actual service in time of War or public danger; nor shall any person be subject for the same offence to be twice put in jeopardy of life or limb; nor shall be compelled in any criminal case to be a witness against himself, nor be deprived of life, liberty, or property, without due process of law; nor shall private property be taken for public use, without just compensation.

6. In all criminal prosecutions, the accused shall enjoy the right to a speedy and public trial, by an impartial jury of the State and district wherein the crime shall have been committed, which district shall have been previously ascertained by law, and to be informed of the nature and cause of the accusation; to be confronted with the witnesses against him; to have compulsory process for obtaining witnesses in his favor, and to have the Assistance of Counsel for his defence.   ·

7. In Suits at common law, where the value in controversy shall exceed twenty dollars, the right of trial by jury shall be preserved, and no fact tried by a jury, shall be otherwise re-examined in any Court of the United States, than according to the rules of the common law.

8. Excessive bail shall not be required, nor excessive fines imposed, nor cruel and unusual punishments inflicted.

9. The enumeration in the Constitution, of certain rights, shall not be construed to deny or disparage others retained by the people.

10. The powers not delegated to the United States by the Constitution, nor prohibited by it to the States, are reserved to the States respectively, or to the people.

The later amendments to the constitution

11. The Judicial power of the United States shall not be construed to extend to any suit in law or equity, commenced or prosecuted against one of the United States by Citizens of another State, or by Citizens or Subjects of any Foreign State. *Passed by Congress March 4, 1794. Ratified February 7, 1795.*

12. The Electors shall meet in their respective states, and vote by ballot for President and Vice-President, one of whom, at least, shall not be an inhabitant of the same state with themselves; they shall name in their ballots the person voted for as President, and in distinct ballots the person voted for as Vice-President, and they shall make distinct lists of all persons voted for as President, and of all persons voted for as

Vice-President and of the number of votes for each, which lists they shall sign and certify, and transmit sealed to the seat of the government of the United States, directed to the President of the Senate;--The President of the Senate shall, in the presence of the Senate and House of Representatives, open all the certificates and the votes shall then be counted;-- The person having the greatest number of votes for President, shall be the President, if such number be a majority of the whole number of Electors appointed; and if no person have such majority, then from the persons having the highest numbers not exceeding three on the list of those voted for as President, the House of Representatives shall choose immediately, by ballot, the President. But in choosing the President, the votes shall be taken by states, the representation from each state having one vote; a quorum for this purpose shall consist of a member or members from two-thirds of the states, and a majority of all the states shall be necessary to a choice. And if the House of Representatives shall not choose a President whenever the right of choice shall devolve upon them, before the fourth day of March next following, then the Vice-President shall act as President, as in the case of the death or other constitutional disability of the President. The person having the greatest number of votes as Vice-President, shall be the Vice-President, if such number be a majority of the whole number of Electors appointed, and if no person have a =majority, then from the two highest numbers on the list, the Senate shall choose the Vice-President; a quorum for the purpose shall consist of two-thirds of the whole number of Senators, and a majority of the whole number shall be necessary to a choice. But no person constitutionally ineligible to the office of President shall be eligible to that of Vice-President of the United States.

passed by Congress December 9, 1803. Ratified July 27, 1804.

13. Section 1.

Neither slavery nor involuntary servitude, except as a punishment for crime whereof the party shall have been duly convicted, shall exist within the United States, or any place subject to their jurisdiction.

Passed by Congress January 31, 1865. Ratified December 6, 1865.

14. Section 1.

All persons born or naturalized in the United States, and subject to the jurisdiction thereof, are citizens of the United States and of the State wherein they reside. No State shall make or enforce any law which shall abridge the privileges or immunities of citizens of the United States; nor shall any State deprive any person of life, liberty, or property, without due process of law; nor deny to any person within its jurisdiction the equal protection of the laws.

Section 2.

Representatives shall be apportioned among the several States according to their respective numbers, counting the whole number of persons in each State, excluding Indians not taxed. But when the right to vote at any election for the choice of electors for President and Vice President of the United States, Representatives in Congress, the Executive and Judicial officers of a State, or the members of the Legislature thereof, is denied to any of the male inhabitants of such State, being twenty-one years of age, and citizens of the United States, or in any way abridged, except for participation in rebellion, or other crime, the basis of representation therein shall be reduced in the proportion which the number of such male citizens shall bear to the whole number of male citizens twenty-one years of age in such State.

Section 3.

No person shall be a Senator or Representative in Congress, or elector of President and Vice President, or hold any office, civil or military, under the United States, or under any State, who, having previously taken an oath, as a member of Congress, or as an officer of the United States, or as a member of any State legislature, or as an executive or judicial officer of any State, to support the Constitution of the United States, shall have engaged in insurrection or rebellion against the same, or given aid or comfort to the enemies thereof. But Congress may by a vote of two-thirds of each House, remove such disability.

Section 4.
The validity of the public debt of the United States, authorized by law, including debts incurred for payment of pensions and bounties for services in suppressing insurrection or rebellion, shall not be questioned. But neither the United States nor any State shall assume or pay any debt or obligation incurred in aid of insurrection or rebellion against the United States, or any claim for the loss or emancipation of any slave; but all such debts, obligations and claims shall be held illegal and void.

Section 5.
The Congress shall have power to enforce, by appropriate legislation, the provisions of this article.
Passed by Congress June 13, 1866. Ratified July 9, 1868

15. Section 1.
The right of citizens of the United States to vote shall not be denied or abridged by the United States or by any State on account of race, color, or previous condition of servitude--

Section 2.
The Congress shall have power to enforce this article by appropriate legislation--
Passed by Congress February 26, 1869. Ratified February 3, 1870.

16. The Congress shall have power to lay and collect taxes on incomes, from whatever source derived, without apportionment among the several States and without regard to any census or enumeration.
Passed by Congress July 2, 1909. Ratified February 3, 1913.

17. The Senate of the United States shall be composed of two senators from each State, elected by the people thereof, for six years; and each Senator shall have one vote. The electors

in each State shall have the qualifications requisite for electors of the most numerous branch of the State legislature.

When vacancies happen in the representation of any State in the Senate, the executive authority of such State shall issue writs of election to fill such vacancies: Provided, That the legislature of any State may empower the executive thereof to make temporary appointments until the people fill the vacancies by election as the legislature may direct.

This amendment shall not be so construed as to affect the election or term of any senator chosen before it becomes valid as part of the Constitution.
Passed by Congress May 13, 1912. Ratified April 8, 1913.

18. After one year from the ratification of this article, the manufacture, sale, or transportation of intoxicating liquors within, the importation thereof into, or the exportation thereof from the United States and all territory subject to the jurisdiction thereof for beverage purposes is hereby prohibited.

The Congress and the several States shall have concurrent power to enforce this article by appropriate legislation.

This article shall be inoperative unless it shall have been ratified as an amendment to the Constitution by the legislatures of the several States, as provided in the Constitution, within seven years from the date of the submission hereof to the States by Congress.
Passed by Congress December 18, 1917. Ratified January 16, 1919. Repealed by Amendment 21

19. The right of citizens of the United States to vote shall not be denied or abridged by the United States or by any States on account of sex.

The Congress shall have power by appropriate legislation to enforce the provisions of this article.
Passed by Congress June 4, 1919. Ratified August 18, 1920.

20. Section 1.

The terms of the President and Vice-President shall end at noon on the twentieth day of January, and the terms of Senators and Representatives at noon on the third day of January, of the years in which such terms would have ended if this article had not been ratified; and the terms of their successors shall then begin.

Section 2.

The Congress shall assemble at least once in every year, and such meeting shall begin at noon on the third day of January, unless they shall by law appoint a different day.

Section 3.

If, at the time fixed for the beginning of the term of the President, the President-elect shall have died, the Vice-President-elect shall become President. If a President shall not have been chosen before the time fixed for the beginning of his term, or if the President-elect shall have failed to qualify, then the Vice-President-elect shall act as President until a President shall have qualified; and the Congress may by law provide for the case wherein neither a President-elect nor a Vice-President-elect shall have qualified, declaring who shall then act as President, or the manner in which one who is to act shall be selected, and such person shall act accordingly until a President or Vice-President shall have qualified.

Section 4.

The Congress may by law provide for the case of the death of any of the persons from whom the House of Representatives may choose a President whenever the right of choice shall have devolved upon them, and for the case of the death of any of the persons from whom the Senate may choose a Vice-President whenever the right of choice shall have devolved upon them.

Section 5.
Sections 1 and 2 shall take effect on the 15th day of October following the ratification of this article.

Section 6.
This article shall be inoperative unless it shall have been ratified as an amendment to the Constitution by the legislatures of three-fourths of the several States within seven years from the date of its submission.

21. Section 1.
The eighteenth article of amendment_to the Constitution of the United States is hereby repealed.

Section 2.
The transportation or importation into any State, Territory, or possession of the United States for delivery or use therein of intoxicating liquors, in violation of the laws thereof, is hereby prohibited.

Section 3.
The article shall be inoperative unless it shall have been ratified as an amendment to the Constitution by conventions in the several States, as provided in the Constitution, within seven years from the date of the submission hereof to the States by the Congress.
Passed by Congress February 20, 1933. Ratified December 5, 1933.

22. Section 1.
No person shall be elected to the office of the President more than twice, and no person who has held the office of President, or acted as President for more than two years of a term to which some other person was elected President shall be elected to the office of the President more than once. But this Article shall not apply to any person holding the office of President when this Article was proposed by the Congress, and shall not prevent any person who May be holding the office of President, or acting as President, during the term

within which this Article becomes operative from holding the office of President or acting as President during the remainder of such term.

Section 2.
This article shall be inoperative unless it shall have been ratified as an amendment to the Constitution by the legislatures of three-fourths of the several States within seven years from the date of its submission to the States by the Congress.
Passed by Congress March 21, 1947. Ratified February 27, 1951.

23. Section 1.
The District constituting the seat of government of the United States shall appoint in such manner as the Congress may direct: A number of electors of President and Vice President equal to the whole number of Senators and Representatives in Congress to which the District would be entitled if it were a state, but in no event more than the least populous State; they shall be in addition to those appointed by the States, but they shall be considered, for the purposes of the election of President and Vice President, to be electors appointed by a State; and they shall meet in the district and perform such duties as provided by the twelfth article of amendment.

Section 2.
The Congress shall have power to enforce this article by appropriate legislation.
Passed by Congress June 16, 1960. Ratified March 29, 1961.

24. Section 1.
The right of citizens of the United States to vote in any primary or other election for President or Vice President, for electors for President or Vice President, or for Senator or Representative in Congress, shall not be denied or abridged by the United States or any State by reason of failure to pay any poll tax or other tax.

Section 2.
The Congress shall have power to enforce this article by appropriate legislation.
Passed by Congress August 27, 1962. Ratified January 23, 1964.

25. Section 1.
In case of the removal of the President from office or of his death or resignation, the Vice President shall become President.

Section 2.
Whenever there is a vacancy in the office of the Vice President, the President shall nominate a Vice President who shall take office upon confirmation by a majority vote of both Houses of Congress.

Section 3.
Whenever the President transmits to the President pro tempore of the Senate and the Speaker of the House of Representatives his written declaration that he is unable to discharge the powers and duties of his office, and until he transmits to them a written declaration to the contrary, such powers and duties shall be discharged by the Vice President as Acting President.

Section 4.
Whenever the Vice President and a majority of either the principal officers of the executive departments or of such other body as Congress may by law provide, transmit to the President pro tempore of the Senate and the Speaker of the House of Representatives their written declaration that the President is unable to discharge the powers and duties of his office, the Vice President shall immediately assume the powers and duties of the office as Acting President.

Thereafter, when the President transmits to the President pro tempore of the Senate and the Speaker of the House of Representatives his written declaration that no inability exists, he shall resume the powers and duties of his office unless the Vice President and a majority of either the principal officers of the executive department or of such other body as Congress may by law provide, transmit within four day to the President pro tempore of the Senate and the Speaker of the House of Representatives their written declaration that the President is unable to discharge the powers and duties of his office. Thereupon Congress shall decide the issue, assembling within forty-eight hours for that purpose if not in session. If the Congress, within twenty-one days after receipt of the latter written declaration, or, if Congress is not in session, within twenty-one days after Congress is required to assemble, determines by two-thirds vote of both Houses that the President is unable to discharge the powers and duties of his office, the Vice President shall continue to discharge the same as Acting President; otherwise, the President shall resume the powers and duties of his office.

Passed by Congress July 6, 1965. Ratified February 10, 1967.

26. Section 1.
    The right of citizens of the United States, who are eighteen years of age or older, to vote shall not be denied or abridged by the United States or by any State on account of age.

    Section 2.
    The Congress shall have power to enforce this article by appropriate legislation.
    Passed by Congress March 23, 1971. Ratified June 30, 1971.

27. No law, varying the compensation for the services of the Senators and Representatives, shall take effect, until an election of Representatives shall have intervened.
    Passed by Congress September 25, 1789. Ratified May 7, 1992.

There are many excellent websites that feature the Bill of Rights and other amendments to the Constitution, and provide information about their history and meaning. This is a particularly good one:

http://www.let.rug.nl/usa/documents/1786-1800/bill-of-rights-and-the-amendments-to-the-constitution.php

THE DECLARATION OF INDEPENDENCE

IN CONGRESS, July 4, 1776.

The unanimous Declaration of the thirteen united States of America,

When in the Course of human events, it becomes necessary for one people to dissolve the political bands which have connected them with another, and to assume among the powers of the earth, the separate and equal station to which the Laws of Nature and of Nature's God entitle them, a decent respect to the opinions of mankind requires that they should declare the causes which impel them to the separation.

We hold these truths to be self-evident, that all men are created equal, that they are endowed by their Creator with certain unalienable Rights, that among these are Life, Liberty and the pursuit of Happiness.--That to secure these rights, Governments are instituted among Men, deriving their just powers from the consent of the governed, --That whenever any Form of Government becomes destructive of these ends, it is the Right of the People to alter or to abolish it, and to institute new Government, laying its foundation on such principles and organizing its powers in such form, as to them shall seem most likely to effect their Safety and Happiness. Prudence, indeed, will dictate that Governments long established should not be changed for light and transient causes; and accordingly all experience hath shewn, that mankind are more disposed to suffer, while evils are sufferable, than to right themselves by abolishing the forms to which they are accustomed. But when a long train of abuses and usurpations, pursuing invariably the same Object evinces a design to reduce them under absolute Despotism, it is their right, it is their duty, to throw off such Government, and to provide new Guards for their future security.--Such has been the patient sufferance of these Colonies; and such is now the necessity which constrains them to alter their former Systems of Government. The history of the present King of Great Britain is a history of repeated injuries and usurpations, all having in direct object the establishment of an absolute Tyranny over these States. To prove this, let Facts be submitted to a candid world.

He has refused his Assent to Laws, the most wholesome and necessary for the public good.

He has forbidden his Governors to pass Laws of immediate and pressing importance, unless suspended in their operation till his Assent should be obtained; and when so suspended, he has utterly neglected to attend to them.

He has refused to pass other Laws for the accommodation of large districts of people, unless those people would relinquish the right of Representation in the Legislature, a right inestimable to them and formidable to tyrants only.

He has called together legislative bodies at places unusual, uncomfortable, and distant from the depository of their public Records, for the sole purpose of fatiguing them into compliance with his measures.

He has dissolved Representative Houses repeatedly, for opposing with manly firmness his invasions on the rights of the people.

He has refused for a long time, after such dissolutions, to cause others to be elected; whereby the Legislative powers, incapable of Annihilation, have returned to the People at large for their exercise; the State remaining in the mean time exposed to all the dangers of invasion from without, and convulsions within.

He has endeavoured to prevent the population of these States; for that purpose obstructing the Laws for Naturalization of Foreigners; refusing to pass others to encourage their migrations hither, and raising the conditions of new Appropriations of Lands.

He has obstructed the Administration of Justice, by refusing his

Assent to Laws for establishing Judiciary powers.

He has made Judges dependent on his Will alone, for the tenure of their offices, and the amount and payment of their salaries.

He has erected a multitude of New Offices, and sent hither swarms of Officers to harrass our people, and eat out their substance.

He has kept among us, in times of peace, Standing Armies without the Consent of our legislatures.

He has affected to render the Military independent of and superior to the Civil power.

He has combined with others to subject us to a jurisdiction foreign to our constitution, and unacknowledged by our laws; giving his Assent to their Acts of pretended Legislation:

For Quartering large bodies of armed troops among us:

For protecting them, by a mock Trial, from punishment for any Murders which they should commit on the Inhabitants of these States:

For cutting off our Trade with all parts of the world:

For imposing Taxes on us without our Consent:

For depriving us in many cases, of the benefits of Trial by Jury:

For transporting us beyond Seas to be tried for pretended offences

For abolishing the free System of English Laws in a neighbouring Province, establishing therein an Arbitrary government, and enlarging its Boundaries so as to render it at once an example and fit instrument for introducing the same absolute rule into these Colonies:

For taking away our Charters, abolishing our most valuable Laws, and altering fundamentally the Forms of our Governments:

For suspending our own Legislatures, and declaring themselves invested with power to legislate for us in all cases whatsoever.

He has abdicated Government here, by declaring us out of his Protection and waging War against us.

He has plundered our seas, ravaged our Coasts, burnt our towns, and destroyed the lives of our people.

He is at this time transporting large Armies of foreign Mercenaries to compleat the works of death, desolation and tyranny, already begun with circumstances of Cruelty & perfidy scarcely paralleled in the most barbarous ages, and totally unworthy the Head of a civilized nation.

He has constrained our fellow Citizens taken Captive on the high Seas to bear Arms against their Country, to become the executioners of their friends and Brethren, or to fall themselves by their Hands.

He has excited domestic insurrections amongst us, and has

endeavoured to bring on the inhabitants of our frontiers, the merciless Indian Savages, whose known rule of warfare, is an undistinguished destruction of all ages, sexes and conditions.

In every stage of these Oppressions We have Petitioned for Redress in the most humble terms: Our repeated Petitions have been answered only by repeated injury. A Prince whose character is thus marked by every act which may define a Tyrant, is unfit to be the ruler of a free people.

Nor have We been wanting in attentions to our Brittish brethren. We have warned them from time to time of attempts by their legislature to extend an unwarrantable jurisdiction over us. We have reminded them of the circumstances of our emigration and settlement here. We have appealed to their native justice and magnanimity, and we have conjured them by the ties of our common kindred to disavow these usurpations, which, would inevitably interrupt our connections and correspondence. They too have been deaf to the voice of justice and of consanguinity. We must, therefore, acquiesce in the necessity, which denounces our Separation, and hold them, as we hold the rest of mankind, Enemies in War, in Peace Friends.

We, therefore, the Representatives of the united States of America, in General Congress, Assembled, appealing to the Supreme Judge of the world for the rectitude of our intentions, do, in the Name, and by Authority of the good People of these Colonies, solemnly publish and declare, That these United Colonies are, and of Right ought to be Free and Independent States; that they are Absolved from all Allegiance to the British Crown, and that all political connection between them and the State of Great Britain, is and ought to be totally dissolved; and that as Free and Independent States, they have full Power to levy War, conclude Peace, contract Alliances, establish Commerce, and to do all other Acts and Things which Independent States may of right do. And for the support of this Declaration, with a firm reliance on the protection of divine Providence, we mutually pledge to each other our Lives, our Fortunes and our sacred Honor.

Signed:

Georgia:
Button Gwinnett
Lyman Hall
George Walton

North Carolina:
William Hooper
Joseph Hewes
John Penn
South Carolina:
Edward Rutledge
Thomas Heyward, Jr.
Thomas Lynch, Jr.
Arthur Middleton

Massachusetts:

John Hancock

Maryland:
Samuel Chase
William Paca
Thomas Stone
Charles Carroll of Carrollton
Virginia:

George Wythe
Richard Henry Lee
Thomas Jefferson
Benjamin Harrison
Thomas Nelson, Jr.
Francis Lightfoot Lee
Carter Braxton

Pennsylvania:
Robert Morris
Benjamin Rush
Benjamin Franklin
John Morton
George Clymer
James Smith
George Taylor
James Wilson
George Ross
Delaware:
Caesar Rodney
George Read
Thomas McKean

New York:
William Floyd
Philip Livingston
Francis Lewis
Lewis Morris

New Jersey:
Richard Stockton
John Witherspoon
Francis Hopkinson
John Hart
Abraham Clark

New Hampshire:
Josiah Bartlett
William Whipple
Massachusetts:
Samuel Adams
John Adams
Robert Treat Paine
Elbridge Gerry
Rhode Island:
Stephen Hopkins
William Ellery
Connecticut:
Roger Sherman
Samuel Huntington
William Williams
Oliver Wolcott
New Hampshire:
Matthew Thornton

There are many excellent websites that feature the Declaration of Independence and provide information about its history and meaning. This is a particularly good one:

http://www.archives.gov/exhibits/charters/print_friendly.html?page=declaration_transcript_content.html&title=NARA%20%7C%20The%20Declaration%20of%20Independence%3A%20A%20Transcription